THE FIRST CHRISTIAN LETTERS

CASCADE COMPANIONS

The Christian theological tradition provides an embarrassment of riches: from Scripture to modern scholarship, we are blessed with a vast and complex theological inheritance. And yet this feast of traditional riches is too frequently inaccessible to the general reader.

The Cascade Companions series addresses the challenge by publishing books that combine academic rigor with broad appeal and readability. They aim to introduce nonspecialist readers to that vital storehouse of authors, documents, themes, histories, arguments, and movements that comprise this heritage with brief yet compelling volumes.

A SELECTION OF TITLES IN THIS SERIES:

Reading Mark by Kelly R. Iverson
Reading Luke by Frank Dicken
Reading John by Christopher W. Skinner
Jesus and the Empire of God by Warren Carter
Reading Acts by Joshua W. Jipp
Reading 1 Corinthians by J. Brian Tucker
Reading Philippians by Nijay K. Gupta
A Companion to Philemon by Lewis Brogdon
A Companion to the Book of Revelation by David L. Mathewson
The Canaanites by Mary Ellen Buck
David: A Man after God's Own Heart by Benjamin J. M. Johnson
The Book of the Twelve by Beth M. Stovell and David J. Fuller
Amos, Hosea, and Micah by Jack R. Lundbom
The Rule of Faith by Everett Ferguson
The Second-Century Apologists by Alvyn Pettersen
Origen by Ronald E. Heine
Practicing Lament by Rebekah Eklund
A Primer in Ecotheology by Celia Deane-Drummond
The Imago Dei by Lucy Peppiatt
Cascade Companion to Evil by Charles Taliaferro
Handel's Messiah by Gregory S. Athnos

THE FIRST CHRISTIAN LETTERS

Reading 1 and 2 Thessalonians

RAFAEL RODRÍGUEZ

 CASCADE *Books* · Eugene, Oregon

THE FIRST CHRISTIAN LETTERS
Reading 1 and 2 Thessalonians

Copyright © 2024 Rafael Rodríguez. All rights reserved. Except for brief quotations in critical publications or reviews, no part of this book may be reproduced in any manner without prior written permission from the publisher. Write: Permissions, Wipf and Stock Publishers, 199 W. 8th Ave., Suite 3, Eugene, OR 97401.

Cascade Books
An Imprint of Wipf and Stock Publishers
199 W. 8th Ave., Suite 3
Eugene, OR 97401

www.wipfandstock.com

PAPERBACK ISBN: 978-1-6667-4869-7
HARDCOVER ISBN: 978-1-6667-4870-3
EBOOK ISBN: 978-1-6667-4871-0

Cataloguing-in-Publication data:

Names: Rodríguez, Rafael, 1977– [author].

Title: The first Christian letters : reading 1 and 2 Thessalonians / by Rafael Rodríguez.

Description: Eugene, OR: Cascade Books, 2024 | Series: Cascade Companions | Includes bibliographical references.

Identifiers: ISBN 978-1-6667-4869-7 (paperback) | ISBN 978-1-6667-4870-3 (hardcover) | ISBN 978-1-6667-4871-0 (ebook)

Subjects: LCSH: Bible.—Thessalonians—Criticism, interpretation, etc. | Bible.—Thessalonians—Commentaries. | Paul, the Apostle, Saint. | Church history—Primitive and early church, ca. 30–600.

Classification: BS2725.53 R63 2024 (paperback) | BS2725.53 (ebook)

VERSION NUMBER 02/09/24

Unless otherwise indicated, Scripture translations are the author's own.

Scripture quotations labelled NRSVue are from the New Revised Standard Version Updated Edition, copyright © 2021 National Council of the Churches of Christ in the United State of America. Used by permission. All rights reserved worldwide.

CONTENTS

Preface | vii
Abbreviations | xi
The First Letter to the Thessalonians | xiii
The Second Letter to the Thessalonians | xx

1 Junk Mail: The Thessalonian Letters in the New Testament | 1

2 Christianity: Faith and *Ethnē* | 16

3 Family: The Gift and Burden of Belonging to Each Other | 34

4 From Charity to Sex: Ethics for a Multi-Ethnic Assembly | 53

5 Visions of the Future: This Ambiguous Thing Called "Eschatology" | 72

6 "A letter claiming to be from us": Paul's Second Letter to the Thessalonians? | 92

7 Hospitality: Welcoming Another as an Other | 113

8 A World Unimaginable: The Thessalonian Letters as the Word of God | 133

Works Cited | 153

PREFACE

THE WORLD CHANGED DRAMATICALLY in the early months of 2020. I was on sabbatical at Johnson University, and I wanted to write a book on the theology and social science of love, though I am neither a theologian nor a social scientist. I was reading works by social psychologists, economists, and political scientists, and I was learning a *lot*, but I had no idea how to organize what I was learning. I couldn't find a way into the book I wanted to write. I couldn't even figure out its major parts.

Then the world shut down. For two weeks. To flatten the curve.

I watched my colleagues transfer all their pedagogical energies onto online platforms, with some beginning to wonder if Zoom might be 2 Thessalonians' "man of lawlessness." I watched them pastor and educate students through the most unpredictable semester in living memory. My sabbatical ended early as we scrambled to prepare for the fall, which—in addition to face masks, enforced social distancing, and mandatory disinfecting—saw us launch a new Bible and Theology curriculum.

As part of that new curriculum, I began teaching a one-semester survey of the entire New Testament. Teaching the four Gospels in five weeks was challenging, but at least I was able to orient myself to the task. As we turned to

Paul's letters, I was confident they wouldn't be too difficult; Romans, after all, is Paul's most difficult letter, and I had already published two books on Romans.[1]

I began with Paul's oldest surviving letters—1 and 2 Thessalonians—and right away I realized these letters were more profound than I had previously realized. I knew they had a lot to say about end times and eschatology (see chapter 5), but I had not realized how these letters speak to a community at odds with but also concerned for the world around it.

So I decided to study the Thessalonian letters. I began working on my own translation, which for the most part follows the text of the NA^{28}. I read introductory works, commentaries, and specialized studies of these letters. I accepted an invitation to write the study notes on 1–2 Thessalonians for a forthcoming study Bible, and, besides this book, I have two other projects on the Thessalonian letters in the works.

I still have a lot to learn. This book, however, reports what I've learned so far. This is not a commentary. It will not discuss all of 1–2 Thessalonians, verse-by-verse or even paragraph-by-paragraph. If you're looking for a good commentary on the Thessalonian correspondence, I recommend the commentaries by Abraham Malherbe (for those able or willing to wade through technical discussions and references to primary sources) and Timothy Brookins (for those looking for a less technical but still rigorous discussion of the text in its historical and theological contexts).[2] These, of course, are not the only good commentaries available.

---

1. Rodríguez, *If You Call Yourself a Jew*; Rodríguez and Thiessen, eds., *So-Called Jew*.

2. Malherbe, *Letters to the Thessalonians*; Brookins, *Thessalonians*.

Preface

Rather than comment on each verse, this book asks, Why should 1–2 Thessalonians be part of the Christian canon? Why should these most ancient of Christian writings have anything at all to say to the complex challenges of being the faithful church in a messy, broken world? What do these easy-to-neglect letters have to say about God, the world, us, and the problem of other people inhabiting the world with us? What kinds of questions are readers—especially Christian readers—encouraged to ask from 1–2 Thessalonians, and what kinds of answers do these letters offer?

I wrote this book for eight-week small groups, book clubs, and Bible studies. While I hope this volume interests undergraduate or graduate students, I wrote it for readers other than full-time students, who maybe can't tell you the difference between a Macedonian or an Achaean, which of Paul's letters are disputed or undisputed, or even what a Thessalonian *is*. I hope this book sparks a curiosity in these letters because—it turns out—they *really are* interesting.

Many people helped me write this book. My closest communities come from two institutions in Knoxville, Tennessee: Johnson University, where I live and work, and Crossings, where I worship. During the summer of 2023, friends and colleagues participated in a Summer Session Group that discussed these letters. Some of the following have read drafts of part or all of this manuscript, but all have helped me think about 1–2 Thessalonians: Amanda and Matthew Broaddus, Austin Bromley, Marcus and Sarah Cathey, Trevor Egli, Andrew Fultz, Caleb Gilmore, Heather Gorman, Rachel Grindle, Jess Hale, Jason and Kealy Mead, Monica Nelson, Nathan Shedd, Tim Sutherland, Josh Wilson, and Jeff and Katie Wischkaemper. John Ketchen and Gary Weedman graciously read drafts of every chapter and met with me over coffee to talk about this project. My wife, Andrea, and two of my parents, Greg and Patti Sommervold, also provided helpful feedback. Kole Barger helped with the final preparation of the manuscript. Chico Dupas, Mitchell Russell, and the staff and patrons of Ebony and Ivory Brewing provided a welcoming space for conversation and community. To all of you: Thank you.

I am grateful to Wipf and Stock for their enthusiastic response when I asked about writing "something about Thessalonians" for Cascade Companions. I hope this is a worthy addition to that wonderful series. I want to mention Chris Spinks, whose friendship made me want to write for Companions, and Robin Parry, who has always been patient with me even when I didn't follow the directions (and I think is the only person who has used the word *rad* in an email to me). Thank you, Chris and Robin.

Some final comments. First, translations of ancient texts are mine unless otherwise noted. Second, in the translations of 1 and 2 Thessalonians that immediately follow this preface, I have *italicized* English words that I added to complete the sense of the Greek. I did not italicize these words in the chapters following the translations. Third, the Greek word *parousia* means "presence," the opposite of *apousia*, "absence." *Parousia* is often translated "coming" or "arrival," which is fine, but in this book I have left *parousia* untranslated. Finally, Paul never referred to himself or anyone else as a *Christian*; as far as we know, he never used the word. Scholars hesitate—even refuse—to use the word in order to avoid portraying Paul and his contemporaries in ways he might not have accepted. In contemporary usage, the word *Christian* denotes a member of a particular religion (Christianity) and excludes members of other religions (esp. Jews). I will never use the word this way. My use of *Christian* only refers to followers of Christ—whether Jews, non-Jews, or both—and *never* distinguishes followers of Christ from Jews. As I use it, *Christian* denotes faith in or allegiance to Jesus as Messiah and excludes neither Jews nor non-Jews.

ABBREVIATIONS

1QS	"The Community Rule," in Vermes, *The Complete Dead Sea Scrolls in English*
AB	Anchor Bible
ABD	*The Anchor Bible Dictionary*
Civ.	Augustine, *The City of God*
DPL[2]	*Dictionary of Paul and His Letters*. 2nd ed. Downers Grove, IL: IVP Academic, 2023
JBL	*Journal of Biblical Literature*
JSNT	*Journal for the Study of the New Testament*
LSTS	The Library of Second Temple Studies
NA[28]	*Novum Testamentum Graece*, 28th ed
NIGTC	The New International Greek Testament Commentary
NTL	The New Testament Library
PCNT	Paideia Commentaries on the New Testament
SNTSMS	Society for New Testament Studies Monograph Series

WUNT	Wissenschaftliche Untersuchungen zum Neuen Testament

THE FIRST LETTER TO THE THESSALONIANS

GREETING

1 Paul and Silvanus and Timothy.
To the assembly of the Thessalonians in God the Father and the Lord Jesus Christ.
Grace and peace to you.

GRATITUDE FOR THE THESSALONIANS

[2] We thank God always for all of you when we make mention of you in our prayers, ceaselessly [3] remembering the work of your faith, the labor of your love, and the endurance of your hope in our Lord Jesus Christ, in the presence of our God and Father, [4] for we are certain—brothers and sisters, beloved by God—of your election, [5] that our gospel did not come to you merely with speech but also with power and with the holy Spirit, and with considerable certainty. Surely you recall what we were like among you, for your sake. [6] So you became imitators of us and of the Lord, by receiving the word amid considerable affliction, along with the joy of the holy Spirit [7] so that you became an example for everyone who believes, throughout Macedonia as well as Achaia.

⁸ For the word of the Lord has rung out from you, not only throughout Macedonia and Achaia but in every place, *the news of* your faithfulness to God has gone out, and so we don't need to say anything, ⁹ for they themselves report about us—what kind of reception we received from you, and how you turned to God from idols to serve the living and true God ¹⁰ and to await his Son from the heavens, whom he raised from the dead, Jesus, who rescued us from the coming wrath.

FRANK SPEECH AND FIERCE OPPOSITION

2 As you are well aware, brothers and sisters, the welcome we received from you was not empty, ² but after we had previously suffered and been mistreated—as you well know—by the people of Philippi, we were emboldened by our God to declare to you, with considerable opposition, the gospel of God. ³ Since our exhortation is based neither on error nor on impurity nor on deception, ⁴ but rather as we have been approved by God to be entrusted with the gospel, so we declare, not like those who *aim merely to* please people but *as those who please* God, who examines our hearts. ⁵ For we never came with a flattering message, as you well know, nor with greedy pretense—with God as our witness—⁶ nor did we solicit glory from mere humans, whether from you or from others. ⁷ Though we could have spoken with gravitas, as apostles of Christ, we were instead gentle among you, as a nursing mother who cherishes her own children. ⁸ So as we longed for you, we decided to share with you not only the gospel of God but even our very lives, because you had become very dear to us. ⁹ For you remember, brothers and sisters, our labor and toil: night and day we were at work so that we would not be a burden on you in any way; we proclaimed to you the gospel of God. ¹⁰ You are witnesses—as is God—how devoutly and justly and blamelessly we were among you who believed, [11] as you well know. *We became for each one of you like a father toward his own children,* [12] encouraging you, consoling you, imploring you to walk in a manner worthy of the God who calls you into his own kingdom and glory.

THESSALONIAN FAITH AMID OPPOSITION

[13] And so we also thank God ceaselessly, because when you received the word of God you heard from us, you welcomed it not as a human message but—just as it truly is—as the word of God, which is also at work among you who believe. [14] For you became imitators, brothers and sisters, of the assemblies of God that are in Christ Jesus in the region of Judea, for you suffered the same *kinds of* things even at the hands of your own people, just as they *suffered* even at the hands of *their fellow* Jews, [15] who killed both the Lord Jesus and the prophets, and who drove us out, and so they were not pleasing to God and they were hostile to all peoples, [16] and they prevented us from speaking to the gentiles so that they might be saved; thus they continually fill up their sins. And so wrath will certainly come upon them at the end.

[17] But, brothers and sisters, ever since we were temporarily orphaned from you—in person but not in our heart—we hastened all the more to see your face with considerable desire. [18] We wanted, therefore, to come to you—I, Paul, again and again—and yet Satan prevented us. [19] For what is our hope or joy or crown of boasting—are you not these things?—before our Lord Jesus at his *parousia*? [20] For you are our glory and our joy.

TIMOTHY, THERE AND BACK AGAIN

3 Therefore, when we could stand it no longer, we decided to be left alone in Athens, [2] and we sent Timothy, our brother and co-laborer of God in the gospel of Christ, to strengthen and encourage you for the sake of your faith, [3] so that no one would be shaken by these afflictions. For you yourselves know that we are appointed for this *task*. [4] For even when we were with you, we were telling you ahead of time that we would suffer, just as it happened, as you well know. [5] For this reason, when I, too, could no longer bear it, I sent to inquire about your faith, lest the one who tests had tested you, *too*, and our labor would have been for nothing.

[6] But now that Timothy has returned to us from you and announced to us your faithfulness and love, and that you always remember us kindly, desiring to see us just as we also *desire to see* you, [7] for this reason we were encouraged about you, brothers and sisters, despite all our disappointment and affliction, through your faithfulness, [8] because we now live, if you are standing firm in the Lord. [9] For what thanks can we give back to God about you, for all the joy that we experience because of you in the presence of our God, [10] as we pray night and day beyond all measure that we might see your face and furnish the things that are lacking from your faith?

A BRIEF PRAYER

[11] So may our God and Father himself, and our Lord Jesus, direct our path to you. [12] May the Lord cause you to grow and increase in love for one another and for everyone, just as we *are experiencing* for you, [13] in order to set your hearts blameless in holiness before our God and Father in the *parousia* of our Lord Jesus, with all his holy ones. *Amen.*

The First Letter to the Thessalonians

HOW FAITH ACTS

4 So then, finally, brothers and sisters, we ask you and encourage you in the Lord Jesus, that just as you received from us the way you should walk and please God—as indeed you are *already* walking—so you would progress even further. ² For you know what instructions we gave you through the Lord Jesus.

³ For this is the will of God, *which* sets you apart as holy: that you keep yourselves from sexual immorality, ⁴ for each one of you to keep control of your self in holiness and honor, ⁵ not in lustful passion, like the gentiles who do not know God, ⁶ that no one transgress or defraud in deed their brother or sister, because God is the avenger of all these things, just as we declared to you before and even now solemnly testify. ⁷ For God did not call you for impurity but in holiness. ⁸ For this reason, whoever rejects *this* does not reject human *authority* but rather God, who [also] gives his holy Spirit to you.

⁹ But you do not need anyone to write you about your love for one another, for you yourselves have been instructed by God to love one another; ¹⁰ even *now* you are doing this very thing for all your brothers and sisters throughout all of Macedonia. So we encourage you, brothers and sisters, to progress all the more, ¹¹ to strive to live peaceably, to attend to your own affairs, and to work with your own hands, as we instructed you, ¹² so that you would conduct yourselves with decency toward those outside and would lack for nothing.

JESUS' PAROUSIA

¹³ We do not want you to be ignorant, brothers and sisters, about those who have fallen asleep, lest you grieve like the rest, who have no hope. ¹⁴ For if we believe that Jesus died

and rose, then *we* also *believe* God, through Jesus, will lead those who have fallen asleep *along* with him. [15] For this is what we said to you by the word of the Lord: We who remain alive until the *parousia* of the Lord will in no way precede those who have fallen asleep. [16] The Lord himself—with a command, with the voice of the archangel and the trumpet of God—will descend from heaven, and the dead in Christ will rise up first, [17] and then we who remain alive will be gathered up in the clouds together with them to meet with the Lord in the air. And so we will always be with the Lord. [18] So then, encourage one another with these words.

5 But you do not need to have anything written to you, brothers and sisters, concerning ages and seasons, [2] for you yourselves are well aware that the day of the Lord is coming like a thief at night. [3] Even as they say, "Peace and safety," then destruction suddenly comes upon them, the way labor comes to a pregnant woman, and they will have no means of escape. [4] But you, brothers and sisters, you are not in the dark, lest that day should catch you like a thief. [5] For you are all children of light and children of the day. We are neither of the night nor of the darkness. [6] Therefore, we do not sleep like the others; rather, we keep alert and sober. [7] For those who sleep sleep at night, and those who get drunk get drunk at night. [8] But, since we are of the day, let us remain sober, armed with the breastplate of faith and love, and, for a helmet, the hope of salvation. [9] For God has not appointed us for wrath but for the possession of salvation through our Lord Jesus Christ, [10] who died for us, so that whether we remain alert or whether we sleep, we will live together with him. [11] Therefore, encourage one another, and build *one another* up, *each* one the *next* one, just as you are *already* doing.

HOW FAITH ACTS, PART II

[12] So we ask you, brothers and sisters, to acknowledge those who labor among you and rule over you in the Lord, and who instruct you; [13] respect them beyond all measure, in love, because of their work. Make peace among yourselves. [14] But we urge you, brothers and sisters: instruct the disorderly; console the weary; devote yourselves to the needs of the weak; be patient toward everyone. [15] See to it that no one repays another person evil for evil, but always pursue the good, *both* for one another and for everyone.

[16] Rejoice always.

[17] Pray unceasingly.

[18] In everything give thanks, for this is the will of God in Christ Jesus for you.

[19] Do not quench the Spirit.

[20] Do not reject the prophetic *task*.

[21] Test all things; hold fast to the good; [22] refrain from every appearance of evil.

CLOSING PRAYER AND GREETINGS

[23] May the very God of peace make you completely holy, and may he keep your whole self—spirit and soul and body—blamelessly in the *parousia* of our Lord Jesus Christ. [24] The one who calls you is faithful; he will do even this.

[25] Brothers and sisters, pray *also* for us.

[26] Greet all the brothers and sisters with a holy kiss. [27] I urge you by Lord to have this letter read to all the brothers and sisters.

[28] *May* the grace of our Lord Jesus Christ *be* with you.

THE SECOND LETTER TO THE THESSALONIANS

GREETING

1 Paul and Silvanus and Timothy.

To the assembly of the Thessalonians in God our Father and the Lord Jesus Christ.

² Grace and peace to you from God our Father and the Lord Jesus Christ.

GRATITUDE FOR AND CONFIDENCE IN THE THESSALONIANS

³ We ought always to thank God for you, brothers and sisters, as is fitting, because your faith is flourishing, and the love each of you has for one another is increasing, ⁴ so that we ourselves boast about you among the assemblies of God; *that is, we boast* of your endurance and your faithfulness through every trial and affliction that you have had to endure. ⁵ *This is* proof of God's just judgment—that you were found worthy of the kingdom of God, for which you have also suffered—⁶ since it is just for God to repay those who afflict you with affliction, ⁷ and *to repay* you who are afflicted with rest along with us at the revelation from

heaven of the Lord Jesus with the angels of his power, [8] with a burning flame, giving vengeance to those who neither know God nor obey the gospel of our Lord Jesus, [9] who will pay the penalty of eternal destruction *which comes* from the presence of the Lord and from the glory of his strength, [10] whenever he comes to be glorified by his holy ones and to be marveled at by all those who believed, because our witness was believed by you, *even* on that *very* day. [11] For this reason we also prayed for you, always, that our God would consider you worthy of his calling and would fulfill every desire for goodness and faithful work in power, [12] so that the name of our Lord Jesus would be glorified among you, and you in him, according to the grace of our God and the Lord Jesus Christ.

REMINDER OF PAUL'S MESSAGE

2 So we ask you, brothers and sisters, with regards to the *parousia* of our Lord Jesus Christ and of our gathering together with him, [2] that you not be easily shaken, nor your mind be troubled, neither by a spirit nor a word nor a letter claiming to be from us that alleges that the day of the Lord has *already* come.

[3] Let no one deceive you in any way; *the day of the Lord will not come* until the rebellion comes and the man of lawlessness is revealed—*that is,* the son of destruction, [4] who opposes and exalts himself over every so-called god or deity, for which reason he sits in the sanctuary of God, *even* proclaiming that he himself is a god. [5] Do you not remember that I was saying these things to you when I was still with you? [6] Even now you know what restrains *him*, so that he would be revealed in his own time. [7] For the mystery of lawlessness is already at work, but only until the one who restrains him is removed. [8] Then, at that point, the lawless

one will be revealed, whom the Lord [Jesus] will destroy by the breath of his mouth, whom he will abolish by the appearing of his *parousia*, ⁹ whose *own parousia* will be the result of the working of Satan, with every miracle and *all kinds of* signs and false wonders, ¹⁰ and with every wicked deception for those who are being destroyed, because they did not accept the love of truth, in which case they would be saved. ¹¹ And so, for this reason, God is sending them an agent of deception, so that they will believe what is false ¹² and everyone who did not believe the truth but found pleasure in injustice will be condemned.

PRAYER AND EXHORTATION

¹³ We, then, ought to thank God always for you, brothers and sisters beloved by the Lord, because God chose you as the first fruits for salvation by the consecration of *your* spirit and *your* faithfulness to truth, ¹⁴ for which reasons he [also] called you by our gospel for the possession of the glory of our Lord Jesus Christ.

¹⁵ So then, brothers and sisters, stand firm and hold on to the traditions that you were taught, whether by speech or by a letter from us. ¹⁶ May our Lord Jesus Christ himself, and God our Father, who graciously loved us and gave us eternal comfort and good hope, ¹⁷ encourage your hearts and strengthen *you* by every good work and word.

3 Finally, brothers and sisters, pray for us, so that the word of the Lord would go forth and be glorified, just as *it did* even among you, ² so that we, too, would be delivered from wicked and evil people. For faith is not *evident* to everyone. ³ But the Lord is faithful; he will strengthen you and keep you from evil. ⁴ So we are persuaded by the Lord for you, that you are *already* doing and will do those things that we are commanding *you*. ⁵ May the Lord direct your hearts to the love of God and to the endurance of Christ.

FURTHER INSTRUCTIONS

⁶ But we command you, brothers and sisters, in the name of *our* Lord Jesus Christ, to keep yourselves from every disorderly brother or sister who has forsaken the tradition that they received from us. ⁷ For you yourselves know how you ought to imitate us, *and* that we were not disorderly among you, ⁸ nor did we take bread from anyone without paying for it. Instead, by labor and toil, night and day we were at work so that we would not be a burden on you in any way. ⁹ Not that we did not have the right, but *we labored* so that we could present ourselves to you as an example, for you to imitate us. ¹⁰ For even while we were with you, we gave you this commandment, that if anyone did not want to work, neither should they eat. ¹¹ For we are hearing *reports of* some people among you who live disorderly lives, not keeping busy but rather being busy bodies. ¹² To people like this, we command and encourage in the Lord Jesus Christ, that by working peaceably they might earn their own bread. ¹³ As for you, brothers and sisters, do not grow weary in doing good.

¹⁴ So if anyone does not obey our word through *this* letter, take note of that person and do not associate with them, so that they might be ashamed. ¹⁵ And do not regard *anyone* as an enemy, but consider *everyone* as a sibling. ¹⁶ And may the Lord of peace himself give you peace through everything and in every way. The Lord be with you all.

CLOSING GREETING

¹⁷ *This is* the greeting *I write* in my own hand: From Paul. This is *my* sign in every letter, just as I've written *here*. ¹⁸ *May* the grace of our Lord Jesus Christ *be* with you all.

1

JUNK MAIL

*The Thessalonian Letters
in the New Testament*

In 2021, the United States Postal Service handled 128.9 billion pieces of mail.[1] As the first full year of a global pandemic, 2021 wrought its own havoc on mail in the US; just two years prior, before the era of bending curves and social distancing, the USPS handled 142.6 billion pieces of mail. Two years and one novel coronavirus eliminated 13.7 billion pieces of mail from the USPS system, a decline of over 9.6 percent. *Junk mail*—unsolicited mail like promotional materials and requests for donations—had a similar trend. The USPS reported a marketing mail volume of 66.2 billion in 2021, down from 75.7 billion in 2019 (a drop of over 12.5 percent). These figures do not even include the trillions-plus unwanted emails sent to our inboxes each year. We are,

---

1. Data for this paragraph are taken from https://facts.usps.com/table-facts/, accessed May 19, 2023.

every one of us, flooded with unwanted mail every single day. And we all know how to handle junk mail: the trash can or the deleted folder.

Bibles, however, do not belong in the trash. If you google "how to dispose of an old Bible," you will find advice ranging from restoring, saving, burning, or burying an old Bible, to consolation that it really is okay to throw it away. Some of us don't feel right throwing away a worn, beloved Bible, which suggests something about the Bible as a physical object. I have no qualms throwing away coupons from my local grocery store. But that copy of the Psalms and the New Testament I got from VBS when I was ten? I don't feel right putting it with the old pizza boxes and discarded tin cans.

The Thessalonian letters seem a bit like that old New Testament I got when I was a kid. They, like it, are special and evoke a sense of reverence and respect. But they, like it, are mostly neglected, kept safe on the shelf. (By "safe," I mean "out of the way.") In 1976, New Testament scholar John Elliott complained that another New Testament letter, 1 Peter, "is generally treated as one of the step-children of the NT canon."[2] Not that stepchildren are or should be neglected, but we understand Elliott's point: 1 Peter ain't the Gospel of Matthew. If 1–2 Thessalonians are not quite the overlooked siblings of the New Testament, they are at least among the more easily neglected letters from Paul. More Harry Potter than Dudley Dursley. More Leah than Rachel. The Thessalonian letters ain't Romans. They ain't even Galatians or Philippians.

I might be uncomfortable admitting it, but 1–2 Thessalonians are something like the junk mail of the New Testament. Maybe not unwanted, but definitely unsolicited. Maybe not discarded, but easily ignored. God or the church

2. Elliott, "Rehabilitation," 243.

or somebody apparently wanted these letters in the Bible. I'm not quite sure why, but they seem harmless enough. Like tossing a compact umbrella into your suitcase for a trip to Phoenix: you probably won't need it, but it won't hurt to bring it with you. And who knows? Maybe it'll be useful.

LETTERS AS SCRIPTURE; SCRIPTURE AS LETTERS

Christians are so used to the New Testament that we hardly even notice that our Bible includes other people's mail. Paul's letter to Christians in Rome? Yep. A letter from Jesus' brother, James? Sure. Even Revelation—that strange book some of us pay no attention to and others pay *way too much* attention to—kicks off with letters to seven churches in western Asia. It's a fact rarely noticed: when Christians turn to the Bible, we find letters.

This is not normal. The Jewish Bible, the Tanakh (roughly equivalent to the Protestant Old Testament, though organized differently and subject to very different traditions of interpretation than the Old Testament), contains very little epistolary material.[3] (The Greek word for *letter* [as in "mail"] is *epistolē*, which is why we also call letters in the New Testament *epistles*.) None of the thirty-nine books in the Old Testament is a letter, though they make references to letters. In a few cases, the contents of letters are recorded, as in Jeremiah 29, where we find a letter from Jeremiah, in Jerusalem, to Jewish exiles in Babylon (modern-day Iraq). But for the most part, ancient Israelites—like Jews of later eras—did not consider their mail inspired by God. Neither

---

3. For an interesting and insightful exploration of the different ways Christians and Jews read "the same texts," see Levine and Brettler, *Bible with and without Jesus*.

THE FIRST CHRISTIAN LETTERS

have Muslims, Buddhists, or Hindus.[4] Inspired mail is not common.

So it is a bit surprising that the letters of one ancient Jew, Paul, came to be included among "the scriptures." The earliest Christians began reading Paul's letters alongside "the other scriptures" even before all twenty-seven books of the New Testament were written (see 2 Pet 3:14–18). Other Jewish writers—including the authors of James, 1 Peter, and 2 Peter—may have been following Paul's example when they decided to write letters to Christians in other places. Whether or not Paul, James, or Peter thought the letters they wrote were *scripture*, their readers began to view them as scripture relatively quickly. And that was unusual. In Paul's day, as in our own, no one thought God spoke to them through the mail. No one, that is, except the early Christians. Whether they were reading a richly theological letter like Galatians, or a deeply grateful letter like Philippians, or a thoroughly personal letter like Philemon, the early Christians came to hear God speaking in these letters.

Our challenge is not simply to hear what God was saying to the earliest readers, but also to ask what God might be saying to us. What should we believe about God? about ourselves? about others? about the world we live in, or the future we hope for? And how should we behave, either toward God or toward others? These are the kinds of questions we should expect our sacred writings to provide some guidance for. If 1 and 2 Thessalonians truly are the word of God, then we should expect them to help us with these kinds of questions.[5]

---

4. Mormon scriptural collections include letters among the various kinds of texts included therein.

5. Christians—whether lay, clerical, or academic—mean very different things by the phrase *word of God*. My use of the term simply means that readers expect or hope to hear, in some way, the voice of

As we consider what it means to read someone else's mail as the word of God, we should keep three things in mind. First, letters—whether ancient or modern—are *occasional*. That is, they were written for a specific occasion or circumstance, and they speak to that occasion. Letters "provide a snapshot of a conversation in process," one author has noted.[6] If we want to read a letter well, we need to try to understand the ongoing conversation that is partially recorded in the letter. Who is speaking? To whom? About what? Is the writer consoling or encouraging the audience? Are they persuading their readers to or dissuading them from a certain point of view? Do they answer questions from their readers? Can we detect how either our author or their readers are feeling? Answers to all these questions affect how we read letters, whether daily letters delivered in the mail or scriptural letters found in the Bible.

Second, these letters were not written to us. We are reading someone else's mail, without either the author's or the recipients' knowledge or permission. The letters in the New Testament were written in an ancient kind of Greek, so they look very different from letters printed in our English Bibles. They were written by Jews who were deeply committed to the God of Israel and who identified Jesus as this God's Son, his *Christ* (or *Messiah*; "anointed one"), who rules on his behalf. And Paul's letters at least were written to non-Jewish readers who had become persuaded that Israel's God deserved their worship (some may also have continued to worship other, "pagan" gods of Greece or Rome or

---

God. Some will hear these words as coming directly from God; some will hear them as coming indirectly from God. Some may not be sure these words come from God at all, though perhaps they offer their readers an opportunity to listen for the voice of God in some sense. While I have my views on these questions, my use of the phrase does not exclude other understandings.

6. Gray, *Opening Paul's Letters*, 17–18.

Egypt or Persia, though Paul would not have looked favorably upon this split loyalty). These non-Jews believed that, somehow, Jesus as Israel's Messiah was also *their* lord, and they sought to order their lives in line with his expectations for them. Knowing what those expectations were was not always easy or straightforward. Like his original readers, many contemporary readers of Paul's letters are also non-Jews, but this hardly means his letters speak to us directly. We, unlike Paul's earliest readers, do not live in cities dominated by images of a divinized emperor or the odor of animals slaughtered to gods both native and foreign. Even the very common presence in our world of symbols of Paul's God and of his Christ can make it difficult to appreciate that Paul advocated devotion to the strange deity of a marginal people. Like Mormons in Rome, or Muslims in Salt Lake City, or Hindus in Baghdad, Paul and his readers were minorities in their societies. In this way, they were very much *not* like contemporary Western readers of the New Testament. We will want to keep that in mind.

Third, and finally, we nevertheless read these letters as if they were written *for* us even if they were not written *to* us. For Christians, letters in the New Testament are the word of God, inspired texts through which God communicates to his people and his people listen for his voice. Paul's letters are both his own words for his readers and also God's word for us. They describe the God we worship. They explain his will for us. They tell us who and what we are—this is both good news and bad news—and point us toward who and what we might become. Paul's letters to the Thessalonians speak to the first century; they speak also to the twenty-first century. Their foreign-ness might mean they sound irrelevant, at best, or even outdated. But in a culture rife with conflicting voices clamoring to define right and wrong, truth and lie, many of us long for a voice with more gravitas, less subject to the flow of popular opinion, more likely to outlast even the most viral social media post. So we read these letters—including 1–2 Thessalonians—as letters to us, and we strain to hear the voice not just of Paul but—somehow and in some way—of God himself.

But first, we must hear Paul's words, in Paul's voice, to Paul's intended readers.

GOOD NEWS FROM THE ASIAN EAST INVADES SOUTHEASTERN EUROPE

By the beginning of the third millennium, Christianity is so thoroughly identified with European culture and geopolitics that it is often seen as a European religion. In many ways, Christianity *is* thoroughly European. But it was not always so. Jesus was a Jew from the Middle East, who spent his childhood and most of his adult life in what is today northern Israel. Judea and Galilee were on the eastern edge of the Roman world, sandwiched between Egypt and Syria, in proximity to the friendly independent kingdom of Nabataea and dangerously close to the rival empire of Parthia. For Greeks and Romans, these were strange and exotic lands, whose people observed foreign customs and spoke unintelligible languages. There was nothing European about Christianity in its earliest generation, except that *Hellenism*—the widespread use of Greek as the common language and the influence of Greek culture, politics, and trade—had spread throughout the Middle East.

Conditions for the gospel's invasion into Europe had been set centuries before an angel appeared to a young, unmarried woman with some startling news of a delicate nature. In 586 BCE the Babylonians defeated the kingdom of Judah and forced many of its inhabitants into exile in Babylon. In 539 BCE the Persians (modern-day Iran) conquered Babylon. Under Persian rule, some Jews would return to Jerusalem and Judah, though Jewish presence in Mesopotamia would remain significant at least until the end of the First World War. The Macedonian king Alexander the Great conquered the Persian Empire in 334 BCE. Jerusalem, in the aftermath of Alexander's sudden death, would fall under first Egyptian and then Syrian control as successive Macedonian kings fought over the area south of Syria and north of Sinai. During these years (336–198 BCE) Jews would come or continue to inhabit the areas of Mesopotamia, Syria, and Egypt. According to the legendary Letter of Aristeas, the Torah, or Pentateuch—the first five books of both the Jewish and Christian Bibles—were translated from Hebrew into Greek in Alexandria, a city founded by and named after Alexander the Great, on Egypt's Mediterranean coast. As Rome came increasingly to dominate the eastern Mediterranean in the second and first centuries BCE, Jews moved into—or were forcibly relocated to—areas under Roman control, including the city of Rome. By the first century CE, when Paul was traveling around the eastern Mediterranean and active among churches in modern-day Syria, Turkey, and Greece, Jewish theology and customs (or "ethics") were already widespread outside Judea and were often popular among non-Jews, to the chagrin of many proud Greeks, Romans, and other peoples.[7]

This is the world in which Paul lived and wrote his letters. First Thessalonians is one of the oldest books of the New Testament, perhaps even *the* oldest. Paul and his companions, Silvanus and Timothy, wrote to a community of Christians in the Macedonian city of Thessalonica, just a few weeks or months after leaving them in a hurry. Macedonia is the northern province of Greece, at the northwestern edge of the Aegean Sea and extending westward to the

7. See Stern, *Greek and Latin Authors.*

Adriatic Sea. In other words, Thessalonica is in southeastern Europe. First Thessalonians was written around 50 or 51 CE, suggesting the early Christian movement expanded rapidly to the north and west, from the Middle East into southeastern Europe in less than two decades. The first time Jesus' name appears in the historical record is in a letter written by a Syrian or Judean Jew (Paul) to European Christians (the Thessalonians).[8] First Thessalonians, therefore, is an important witness to the gospel's earliest foray from Asia into Europe.

Unfortunately, 1 Thessalonians does not reveal very much about that foray. Paul and his companions came to Thessalonica from Philippi, about a hundred miles to the east along the Via Egnatia, a road running east-to-west, from the Bosporus Strait (where Europe and Asia meet, in modern-day Istanbul, Turkey) to the Adriatic Sea. They had experienced hard times in Philippi, and more of the same met them in Thessalonica (1 Thess 2:2). The authors engaged in manual labor alongside the Thessalonians as they proclaimed the gospel (2:9). They were able to persuade several non-Jews to abandon the worship of pagan gods and "serve the living and true God," that is, the Jewish God (1:9). Nothing in 1 Thessalonians sounds like the authors wrote to Jewish followers of Jesus, and though the letter does not say how long Paul and his friends were in Thessalonica, most people think the letter implies a stay of at least few months. Whatever the case, they had to leave suddenly, and they have not yet been able to return (2:17–18).

Eventually, while in Athens (about three hundred miles to the south), Paul and Silvanus were able to send Timothy back to make sure the Thessalonians were alright (1 Thess 3:1–5). After making the trip north, Timothy returned to Paul and Silvanus, who were probably in Corinth,

8. See also Rodríguez, *Jesus Darkly*, 7–10.

about fifty miles west of Athens. Timothy reported the Thessalonians were standing firm in their faithfulness to Jesus and to Israel's God, and they remembered Paul and his companions fondly (3:6–10). And so Paul, Silvanus, and Timothy wrote 1 Thessalonians, probably from Corinth, in Achaia (southern Greece), perhaps a mere few weeks or, at most, a couple months after their first visit to Thessalonica.[9]

Perhaps thirty years or so after Paul's first visit to Macedonia and his earliest known letter, an author whose name we do not know compiled an "orderly account" of the life and teaching of Jesus as well as the activities of some of Jesus' earliest followers. This account, found in the Gospel of Luke and the Acts of the Apostles (which together are called Luke-Acts), includes the events of Paul's first journey into Greece: his movements from Philippi to Thessalonica and on to Athens and Corinth (see Acts 15:36—18:22). As Paul and Silas (a shortened form of Silvanus?) traveled westward across Asia Minor, they picked up another companion, Timothy (16:1–5). For whatever reason (Luke-Acts does not say), Paul and his friends were prevented from going into the regions of Asia and Bithynia (southwestern and northwestern Turkey today), so they continued west, to Troas, on the northeastern edge of the Aegean Sea (16:6–10). From there they left western Asia and arrived in southeastern Europe. They started in Macedonia (Philippi, Thessalonica, and Beroea; 16:11—17:14) before moving south to Achaia (Athens and Corinth; 17:15—18:17). Eventually, Paul returned to Jerusalem (in Judea) and Antioch (in Syria), where he stayed for a while before beginning another journey (18:18–23).

The story of Paul in Thessalonica is found in Acts 17:1–9. Paul and the author of Luke-Acts largely agree on the events in this period of Paul's life, though there are

9. See also Ascough, *Thessalonians*.

important differences. For one thing, Luke-Acts places Paul's preaching in "a synagogue of the Jews" and says he was there for "three Sabbaths," or two to three weeks (Acts 17:1–2). The author says, "Some of them were persuaded" by Paul, by which he must mean "some of the Jews" (17:4). The Greek word for "some" does not mean "not many"; it's just undefined. Other Jews get jealous and rile up a mob to oppose Paul and his friends (17:5–7). But Paul's preaching about Jesus also persuaded "a large crowd of devout Greeks, including not just a few elite women" (17:4). Paul's success in Acts among non-Jews ("devout Greeks") matches 1 Thess 1:9, though the connection of these non-Jews to the synagogue is not hinted at in Paul's letter.[10]

Also, in 1 Thessalonians we get the impression that Paul, Silvanus, and Timothy travel together from Thessalonica to Athens; Timothy returns to Thessalonica from Athens and eventually re-joins Paul and Silvanus, perhaps in Corinth (1 Thess 3:1–2, 6). According to Acts, however, Silas (Silvanus?) and Timothy remained in Beroea (Acts 17:14) while Paul traveled (alone?) to Athens. Paul then made his way to Corinth, where he met a Jewish couple, Priscilla and Aquila (18:1–3). Only now—after he has left Athens and gone on to Corinth—do Silas and Timothy join Paul (18:5). According to 1 Thessalonians, Paul and Silvanus sent Timothy back north to Macedonia from Athens. According to Luke-Acts, Paul was without his two companions while in Athens; they joined him later, after he went to Corinth.

While we will need to recognize that Paul and the author of Luke-Acts wrote different texts, for different reasons, to different audiences, with different perspectives, that does not mean we should ignore one as hopelessly inaccurate

10. For a comprehensive discussion of Acts as a source of knowledge for Paul's early period, see Riesner, *Paul's Early Period*.

and rely only on the other. Paul was a direct participant in the events of his arrival and preaching in Thessalonica; the author of Luke-Acts reported on events he heard from others as they fit within his understanding of the church's early history. If and when we find differences between Paul and Luke-Acts, those differences may result from Paul reporting on events he experienced and Luke-Acts reporting events secondhand. Or else they may be signs that we are misreading Paul, Luke-Acts, or both. Inasmuch as Luke-Acts shows us how the events in Thessalonica were remembered a generation after Paul, we will allow Paul and Luke-Acts to guide our interpretation of each other.[11]

A SECOND LOOK AT UNWANTED MAIL

Earlier we raised a series of questions that help orient us to the challenge of reading occasional writings (such as letters) and understanding them well. Who is speaking? To whom? About what? Is the writer consoling or encouraging the audience? Are they persuading their readers to or dissuading them from a certain point of view? Do they answer questions from their readers? Can we detect how either our author or their readers are feeling?

We now have a sense of the main characters in our story: Paul, Silvanus, and Timothy on one hand, writing to non-Jews in Thessalonica who had turned from the native gods of northern Greece to worship the God of Israel and follow a certain "Jesus," the Son of Israel's God. First Thessalonians is not an angry letter (like Galatians); instead, the authors are affectionate toward and grateful for their readers and express confidence that their love is mutual.

---

11. For technical discussions of Acts and Paul, see Charlesworth, "Why Should Experts Ignore Acts," 151–66; and especially White, "Pauline Tradition," 39–53.

There is a hint of concern that the readers are experiencing opposition from others, but the authors are clear that such things are to be expected—they are, after all, followers of a crucified king! Nevertheless, as we will see in a later chapter, our authors urge their readers to be open to and do right by outsiders.[12] The letter repeatedly presents itself as simply a reminder to the readers of things they already know; some form of the phrase "as you well know" occurs nearly ten times in 1 Thessalonians! Even when the authors are offering instructions to the readers to do this or that or to remember something or other, there is hardly any hint that the authors are upset with their readers.

So what are Paul and his companions trying to do in these letters? Part of the answer is simply that the authors want the Thessalonians to know they are not forgotten or abandoned in their current struggles. Neither Paul nor his Jewish God has deserted these non-Jews. Perhaps we could summarize the entire first letter to the Thessalonians as follows:

> We were worried you had given up fighting the good fight, so when we found out you hadn't, we were so relieved. You are all doing so well; keep it up! As you face these new but not unexpected challenges, here are some things for you to keep in mind.

The English text of 1 Thessalonians is about two thousand words long, so this fifty-word summary leaves a lot out. But it's a start.

Still . . . why should we expect these letters to say anything meaningful to *us* as we face our own new but maybe not unexpected challenges? We receive more information in a single day than the average person in Paul's day would

---

12. See chapter 7, below.

receive in an entire lifetime. (I don't know if this is *literally* true, but it's at least *directionally* accurate.) We live in a world defined by political strife and polarization, racial tensions resulting from centuries of abuse, miscommunication, and mistrust. Our social and civic institutions—those groups and gatherings in which we find and forge our connections with others and find meaning beyond ourselves—have been collapsing for over a half-century. Our growing sense of isolation and the related posture of defensiveness that increasingly defines how we interact with others (not just strangers but also friends and, sadly, even family) tear at the social fabric of every level of society: family, work, church, the public square, and everywhere else.[13]

In Paul's world, people traveled slowly and had to expend almost unimaginable effort to communicate with someone not in their immediate presence. In our world, we can travel across continents in a single day and communicate on a whim with someone literally on the other side of the globe. It is difficult to imagine a world less like the eastern Mediterranean during the early Roman Empire than our own.

And yet . . . Paul and his companions' words to the Thessalonian Christians address some of the challenges facing us today. In the following chapters, we will address questions of identity and its intersection with ethnicity and faith (chapter 2), family relations and obligations (chapter 3), assorted ethical questions arising in a multi-ethnic community (chapter 4), our hopes and fears regarding the future (chapter 5), disinformation, authority, and "fake news" (chapter 6), and the challenges and promise of welcoming others amid real and significant difference (chapter 7).

---

13. The classic study is Putnam, *Bowling Alone*, which was revised and updated in 2020. For the political effects of the collapse of social capital, see Carney, *Alienated America*.

There are no guarantees that Paul and his friends will say helpful things to us as we wrestle with very similar questions in our own era, but the topics, at least, are as relevant today as they were then.

Perhaps we will find these letters really are outdated and irrelevant, harmless but not helpful for life in the twenty-first century. Maybe worse, perhaps these texts undermine our striving toward "the good life," however we imagine it. It would be foolish for us to decide now, before we even begin, that these letters *must* speak to today's questions. But in a world often overwhelmed by a flood of information, surrounded by voices whose interests and agenda are not always easily discerned, and not always sure whom we can trust, perhaps a voice from outside our immediate melee might provide us with some perspective and orientation.

There really is only one way to find out. It's time to turn the page.

DISCUSSION QUESTIONS

1. Have you ever read 1–2 Thessalonians? If so, how long ago, and what do you remember of that experience? If not, is there a reason why not?
2. What expectations, questions, or suspicions do you bring to reading these letters, whether for the first time or once again?
3. How do you think you can read letters written for someone else as the word of God that speaks to you? What do you hope to hear? What do you *need* to hear?
4. If God said to you, "You are doing so well; keep it up!" what do you think God would mean? Would you believe him? Why, or why not?

2

CHRISTIANITY

Faith and Ethnē

RACE AND ETHNICITY AS "NARRATIVES OF BELONGING"

THE ENGLISH WORD *NATION* comes from the Latin noun *natio*, "birth," and the verb *nascor*, "I am born." We can see this root, with shades of this meaning, in English words like *nativity*, *prenatal*, and *native*. *Nations* in this sense are groups of people with stories of common ancestry and descent, people who belong together because, in an extended sense, they are family. Moreover, people who descend from a common ancestor often, even typically, have other traits in common. They speak the same language. They worship the same gods. They eat the same foods. They have common ways of raising their children, honoring their dead, rewarding their friends, opposing their enemies, celebrating their past, and so on. Recall the promise God made to Abraham in Genesis: "I will make of you a great nation" (Gen 12:2).

Israel, as Abraham's descendants, share a story of common descent from Abraham, and this story infuses the myriad other traits that bind Israel as a people and distinguish them from other peoples: their language, their religion, and their culture.[1]

What matters is the *story* of common descent, the myth of belonging to a shared ancestor and, by implication, to each other. (By *myth* I do not mean "tale," "legend," or "untrue story." A myth is *a foundational story* that relates events from the significant past and explains how people think about and behave in their world. Those events may be actual or symbolic. Whether they actually happened or not, we use myths to explain ourselves to ourselves.) Ancient Israelites and Jews did not have DNA tests to verify their descent from a common father. But Abrahamic DNA was less important than the *story* of descent from Abraham (and Sarah!). The descendants of Ishmael and Esau also had Abrahamic DNA, but they were not Israel. Ishmael and Esau were outsiders in the story of Abraham and the "great nation" of his descendants, despite being a son and grandson, respectively, of Abraham.

All of this gets us to a significant point: co-members of a nation are part of an *imagined community*.[2] Whether they actually descend from a common ancestor or not, the bonds that bind them as a people exist in their heads and are made real in their interactions with others who think of themselves as belonging to the same imagined community. *Imagined* does not mean *imaginary* or *unreal*. Instead, *imagined* tells us how the bonds of peoplehood get their

---

1. The word *myriad* comes from the Greek *myrias*, literally "ten thousand," but often used more generally, not unlike how we use "thousands" or "millions" (or even "billions") when we mean "a lot."

2. The phrase *imagined community* comes from Anderson, *Imagined Communities*.

power: whether they exist in the world or not, they absolutely exist in their minds. Moreover, stories of common descent are reinforced by aspects of everyday life: a common language, a common religion, a common culture, a common homeland, and much else besides.

People in Paul's day also had to navigate questions about race, nationality, and belonging, just like we do, even if the details differ. And Paul was not that different from other people in his day. We sometimes imagine Paul's Jewish contemporaries were especially xenophobic (wary, even *fearful*, of strangers or foreigners), but the gospel revealed to Paul that God loves *everybody*, irrespective of race, ethnicity, gender, or social status. All of this is surely wrong. Of course, some Jews undoubtedly held what we would call "nationalistic views" in the midst of the pluralist, chaotically multicultural world in the wake of Alexander the Great. But the ancient world also preserves evidence of Jews—perhaps most Jews—finding various ways to live with and among non-Jews, usually quite amicably. In fact, some non-Jewish writers even complain about Jewish influence over their pagan neighbors.[3] Seneca, a contemporary of Paul and tutor of the mad emperor, Nero, was reported to have complained: "the customs of this accursed race (*sceleratissimae gentis*) have gained such influence that they are now received throughout all the world. The vanquished

---

3. For the language of *pagan* and, where appropriate, *ex-pagan* as synonyms for *gentile*, see Fredriksen, *Paul*: "My phrase 'ex-pagan pagans'—by which I mean to describe those non-Jewish members of the first generation of the messianic movement around Jesus—is thus deliberately oxymoronic. The term's inelegance highlights the extreme anomaly, socially and therefore religiously, that this first generation represented: they were non-Jews who, *as* non-Jews, committed themselves to the exclusive worship, in some specifically Jewish ways, of the Jewish god" (34; italics in the original).

have given laws to their victors."[4] Obviously, Seneca was not a fan of the Jews' popularity among their neighbors. But did you notice his complaint that people throughout "all the world" did not, apparently, share his displeasure? Even someone as hostile as Seneca could not help but notice that Jews got on with their neighbors, perhaps all too well.

So Jews were not, on the whole, as xenophobic as some people like to imagine. Okay. But Paul gave up having any pride in being Jewish, right? I mean, Paul himself considered his "Jewish credentials" as "loss," even "bullshit" (Greek: *skybalon*; see Phil 3:4–8). After all, Paul wrote: "There is neither Jew nor Greek; there is neither slave nor free; there is neither male nor female. For all of you are one in Christ Jesus" (Gal 3:28).

Yes, Paul elevated knowing Christ and being known by him above any other aspect of his identity. But we cannot ignore other things Paul wrote. For example, after asking the rhetorical questions, "What, then, is so remarkable about being called a Jew? or, What is the advantage of circumcision," Paul answered, "A great deal, in every respect!" (Rom 3:1–2). Later in the same letter he describes Jews as those "to whom belong the adoption and the glory and the covenants and the law-giving and the temple cult and promises, to whom belong the patriarchs and from whom comes the Christ according to the flesh" (9:3–5).[5] We see, then, that even late in life—Romans was written in 57, perhaps just five years or so before he was killed by Nero—Paul

---

4. Seneca, according to Augustine, *Civ.* 6.11.6–8; see Stern, *Greek and Latin Authors*, 1:431 (§186).

5. The word *cult* (and related forms, including *cultic*) in religious studies refers to "formal religious veneration" (Merriam-Webster) or any system of religious worship, including especially systems of animal or other sacrifices. This is very different than the popular use of *cult* to refer to small, heterodox, dangerous, and/or extremist religious sects.

continued to find immense value in his national identity. Paul's activity among non-Jews, therefore, did not lead him to devalue, denigrate, or despise his own national identity. Just like other Jews in his day, Paul had to navigate a world populated, even *dominated*, by pagan non-Jews; he also continued to ascribe value to his own ethnic and racial identity. As a Jew during the Roman era, Paul's "narrative of belonging" was wholly focused on Abraham (the ancestor of Israel), on YHWH[6] (the God of Israel), on Moses (the covenant law-giver of Israel), on Torah and the Prophets (the scriptures of Israel), and on Jesus as the truest and ultimate expression of Jewish identity. Despite his work among non-Jews, Paul *never* adopted his audiences' "narratives of belonging." He *always* oriented his non-Jewish readers toward an Abrahamic, Jewish "narrative of belonging." That will become important as we turn to Paul's words to the Thessalonians.

A JEWISH LETTER TO NON-JEWS IN THESSALONICA

On first glance, very little about 1 or 2 Thessalonians addresses questions of race and ethnicity.[7] The Greek word *ethnē*, literally "nations" but often translated "gentiles" (or

---

6. The name of God in Hebrew is written using four consonants: *y-h-w-h*. In English, the name of God is often transliterated (YHWH) or translated and printed in small capital letters (Lord). The pronunciation of YHWH is uncertain; some Christians pronounce the name of God as *Yahweh*, while other Christians and Jews substitute the title *the Lord* for YHWH.

7 While everyday speech uses *race* and *ethnicity* roughly synonymously, scholars use the terms to refer to different aspects of a person's or group's identity. In this book, the phrase "race and ethnicity" refers to the overlapping aspects of identity pertaining to genetic descent, familial relation, cultural practice, language, religion, homeland, and so on.

"non-Jews"), pops up in these letters only twice (compare Galatians, where Paul uses the same word ten times!). The word *Ioudaios* ("Jewish person or place") also occurs twice, once to refer to "the Jews" and once to refer to "Judea." In his later letters, Paul frequently (and passionately) addresses questions of gentiles and Jewish theology and practice, but not so much in these early letters. The fact is, in 1–2 Thessalonians, Paul and his companions are not much concerned with the kinds of questions that will dominate future letters.

On closer inspection, however, questions of race and ethnicity are at the heart of this correspondence, in part because questions of race and ethnicity are at the heart of Paul's gospel: both the message he proclaims and his act of proclaiming it.

I mentioned already that the authors use the word *ethnē* (nations/gentiles/non-Jews) twice in the Thessalonian correspondence. First, they complain that non-Christ-following Jews "prevented us from speaking to the gentiles [*ethnē*] so that they might be saved" (1 Thess 2:16). We will return to 1 Thess 2:14–16 shortly, but for now we should note our authors' desire to deliver the message about Jesus specifically to non-Jews. Paul feels a responsibility, even an obligation, to proclaim the gospel of Jesus to non-Jews (*ethnē*; "gentiles or pagans").

This differs considerably from the other use of *ethnē* in 1 Thessalonians. In chapter 4, Paul and Silvanus and Timothy direct their readers away from sexual immorality (Greek: *porneia*): "keep control of your self in holiness and honor, not in lustful passion, like the gentiles [*ethnē*] who do not know God" (4:4–5). Here in 1 Thessalonians 4, the word *gentiles* identifies a pattern of behavior to be avoided. Elsewhere, Paul refers to "gentile sinners" (see Gal 2:15), which fits with his use of word *gentiles* here: gentiles are simultaneously especially prone to moral dysfunction and also the special object of Paul's evangelistic activities. In other words, both the reason for and the target of Paul's preaching are ethnically defined.

Even more important than the word *ethnē*, however, our authors remind their Thessalonian readers about their past, "how you turned to God from idols to serve the living and true God and to await his Son from the heavens" (1 Thess 1:9–10). We can make at least two important observations here. First, and most importantly, our authors imagine themselves writing to Thessalonians who used to worship pagan gods ("idols"). Those pagans, however, have renounced those gods to worship the God of Israel, whom our authors describe as "the living and true God." Even before they met Paul and his companions, the Thessalonians were pious, religious, spiritual. But their piety, from Paul's point of view, was misdirected, aimed at lifeless idols, and for whatever reason the Thessalonians were persuaded by Paul to redirect their religious commitments and activities toward a different God, a foreign God, *Paul's* God. Jesus was a significant part of Paul's proclamation of the gospel; of course he was. But we should not be so distracted by the Thessalonians' faith in Jesus that we miss their reorientation toward Israel's God, Jesus' Father.

Second, our authors do not say *some* of their readers have turned from idolatrous worship of pagan gods to worship Israel's "living and true God." They simply state, plainly and baldly: "*you* turned to God from idols." This is a bit of a problem. On the one hand, as we noted in the previous chapter, nothing in 1 Thessalonians sounds like the authors are addressing or sending greetings to Jewish followers of Jesus. On the other hand, we also noted that Acts—written about a generation after Paul's death—portrays Paul in a synagogue arguing "from the scriptures, explaining and proving that it was necessary for the Messiah to suffer and to rise from the dead" (Acts 17:2–3 NRSVue). So which is it? Are there Jews among the Thessalonian Christians, as claimed by Acts? Or is Paul writing to non-Jews without any connection to an actual Jewish community or synagogue?

When faced with an either/or question like this—*either* accept Acts's portrayal of the Jewish origin of the church in Thessalonica, *or* accept the authors' portrayal of all their readers as ex-pagans—many scholars opt for Paul's letters as more reliable evidence over Acts as a secondhand source. If we follow these scholars, we get a picture of the church in Thessalonica largely unhitched from Christianity's Jewish roots. The Thessalonian letters were written to gentile followers of Christ, who had once worshipped pagan gods from one or more of the gentile pantheons. The Thessalonians' lack of connection to Jewish traditions and theology helps to explain why 1 Thessalonians never cites or quotes from the Jewish scriptures.[8]

This is not how I read either 1 Thessalonians or Acts. It is true that our evidence for a substantial Jewish presence in Thessalonica before the second century is scarce, so it is certainly possible that Acts misrepresents the circumstances of the earliest Thessalonian Christians when it locates Paul's activities in a Jewish synagogue. Even if we accept this scenario, however, we cannot lose sight of the fact that Paul is a *Jewish* writer, an advocate (or emissary) of the *Jewish* God and a *Jewish* messiah. While there is a certain truth to claims that 1 Thessalonians "only sparingly cites Jewish traditions and cultural memories,"[9] we should not forget that every reference in 1 Thessalonians to "God" (*theos*; 36x), "Christ" or "Messiah" (*Christos*; 10x), and God's

---

8. See Ascough, *Paul's Macedonian Associations*, 312; cited by Rollens, "Paul, 1 Thessalonians."

9. Rollens, "Paul, 1 Thessalonians."

"Spirit" (*pneuma*; 4x)[10] are references to *Jewish* theological ideas. The "Christian" faith of Paul's Thessalonian readers is itself evidence of Jewish influence in Thessalonica, whether or not there was a Jewish synagogue in Thessalonica during Paul's lifetime. First Thessalonians itself is evidence that Paul and his companions successfully persuaded some pious pagans to abandon their gods and turn to "the living and true God" of Israel.

Unfortunately, we do not have sufficient evidence to explain *how* Paul managed to persuade these pagans, or *why* these pagans found Paul's message persuasive. One plausible explanation is that Jews in Thessalonica (slaves? merchants?) had already brought traditions about one Creator God to Thessalonica and expounded the traditions of this God in weekly synagogue meetings as well as in whatever aspects of their distinctively Jewish lifestyle were visible to the public. We have already seen that one of Paul's non-Jewish contemporaries, Seneca, regretted the influence of Jewish theology and practice over Romans. Other historical evidence suggests that gentiles often—not always, but often—found Jewish traditions attractive. It is not impossible that Paul arrived in a pagan city without any meaningful or noticeable Jewish presence and nevertheless found a receptive audience for his proclamation of a Jewish messiah. However, that 1 Thessalonians was written so quickly on the heels of Paul's departure from the city makes it likely that there were already Jews in the city before Paul, Silvanus, and Timothy arrived there. A generation or two later, the author of Acts will mention a synagogue in Thessalonica and locate Paul's preaching in that synagogue.

---

10. The word *pneuma* can refer to the "Spirit" of God, often (but not always) described as the "holy Spirit" (see 1 Thess 1:5, 6; 4:8; but see also 5:19), but it can also refer to the "spirit" of a human being, as in 1 Thess 5:23.

Although 1 Thessalonians does not mention a synagogue or other Jewish gathering in the city, we cannot construe the letter's silence as evidence that Thessalonica did not have a synagogue when Paul wrote that letter. The author of Acts and Paul both have their different reasons for writing (and different goals in doing so); these very different authors nevertheless offer consistent images of the ethnic situation in Thessalonica in the mid-first century.

In his later letters, Paul explains that announcing the message of Israel's God and of Israel's Messiah is at the heart of his calling as an apostle. In his letter to the Romans, Paul presents himself as a priest officiating over the gentiles' offering to Israel's God (see Rom 15:15–17). In a bit of an angry letter, Paul explains that even the most significant figures in the first generation of Jesus' followers acknowledged his call to take the gospel to non-Jews, just as Peter and his companions had been called to take the gospel to Jews (see Gal 2:7–9). Paul even refers to himself as the "apostle to the gentiles" (Rom 11:13), which is reflected also in Acts's account of Paul's encounter with the risen Jesus (Acts 9:15; see also 1 Tim 2:7). In other words, there is a fundamentally *ethnic* component to Paul's commission to preach the gospel of Jesus Christ. He is not simply "an apostle," sent out into the world. He is *the* Jewish herald of a Jewish messiah, sent out to nations that are not-Israel to call them from their impotent worship of impotent gods "to serve the living and true God" (1 Thess 1:9).[11]

THE COMMON FAITHFULNESS OF JUDEAN JEWS AND THESSALONIAN NON-JEWS

The most perplexing problem regarding race and ethnicity and 1 Thessalonians is definitely 1 Thess 2:14–16, a passage

11. See Thiessen, *A Jewish Paul*.

that has provoked questions such as, Was Paul antisemitic? Were the Jews responsible for Jesus' crucifixion? Has God rejected the Jews for their role in Jesus' crucifixion? Did Paul even write these verses?[12] These are among the most commented-upon verses in 1 Thessalonians, and we will need to consider them, even if only briefly, before wrapping up our discussion of race/ethnicity and the Thessalonian correspondence. Here is the problematic passage:

> For you became imitators, brothers and sisters, of the assemblies of God that are in Christ Jesus in the region of Judea, for you suffered the same kinds of things even at the hands of your own people, just as they suffered even at the hands of their fellow Jews, who killed both the Lord Jesus and the prophets, and who drove us out, and so they were not pleasing to God and they were hostile to all peoples, and they prevented us from speaking to the gentiles so that they might be saved; thus they continually fill up their sins. And so wrath will certainly come upon them at the end. (1 Thess 2:14–16)

As you can see, these verses lay responsibility for Jesus' execution at the feet of "the Jews" (Greek: *hoi Ioudaioi*) and identifies this behavior as typical for this *ethnos* (Greek for "people" or "nation"): they behaved similarly toward the prophets before Jesus and the apostles after him. These Jews appear uniquely misanthropic, and their misanthropy results in their "continually filling up their sins" and, ultimately, incurring God's wrath.

In the last section we saw that Paul, as the Jewish herald of a Jewish messiah, felt himself fundamentally called to "the nations" (Greek: *ta ethnē*) beyond Israel. These verses raise the question of Paul's view of his own *ethnos*, his own

---

12. See Weatherly, "Authenticity of 1 Thessalonians 2:13–16."

people, the Jews. We should acknowledge that many scholars think these verses were written later, by someone else, perhaps in the margin of a copy of 1 Thessalonians. If so, these verses were accidentally (but erroneously) inserted into the text by a later scribe making a new copy of this letter. For scholars who question whether Paul wrote these verses, the portrayal of "the Jews" contradicts Paul's more optimistic view of "all Israel" in Romans 9–11 (esp. Rom 11:23–32). Moreover, the phrase "wrath will certainly come upon them at the end" sounds like a reference to the Romans' destruction of Jerusalem's temple in 70 CE. But Paul was killed in the 60s, which would make it impossible for Paul to refer to the temple's destruction. We do not have space to address this issue here, but I want to acknowledge the question. For my own part, I accept that Paul wrote these words, and so the end of v. 16 cannot refer to the destruction of the temple.

Whatever we think of the origin of 1 Thess 2:14–16, we need to address the question of Paul's view of his own people, the Jews. This passage, however, is not as problematic as it has been made out to be. For one thing, this paragraph does not denigrate or condemn "the Jews" as a race or a people. Rather, these verses praise the Thessalonian Christians for accepting the gospel as "the word of God" (2:13) and for standing alongside Paul and other Jewish followers of Jesus who are standing firm despite opposition from their neighbors. Far from condemning "the Jews" as a whole, these verses liken the ex-pagan, gentile followers of Jesus in Thessalonica with Jewish followers of Jesus in Judea. The Thessalonians, like their Jewish counterparts in Judea, are embracing and holding fast to their faith in Jesus as Israel's Messiah despite the social and emotional toll of being opposed by friends, family, neighbors, and others in their immediate and daily experience.

In 1 Thess 2:14, the words *they* and *their* ("you suffered the same kinds of things even at the hands of your own people, just as *they* suffered even at the hands of *their* fellow Jews"), refer to Jews just as much as do the words *fellow Jews*. That is, Jewish followers of Jesus suffered at the hands of other Jews, just as Thessalonian gentile followers of Jesus have suffered at the hands of other Thessalonian gentiles. The point here is *not* that gentiles have shown themselves faithful to God while Jews have shown themselves unfaithful. The point is that some gentiles (= non-Jews) have been faithful *just like some Jews* (including Paul, Silvanus, and Timothy!) have been faithful. In these faithful populations—whether Jewish or not—God is demonstrating his persistent faithfulness to obstinate populations—Jewish or otherwise. God has no more disavowed his covenantal relationship with Israel and/or the Jews than he has rejected the rest of humanity as little more than fuel for the white-hot inferno of his eschatological wrath. While there is a clear and significant ethnic dimension to these verses, they do not express God's preference for one or more nations (Greek: *ethnē*) at the expense of another (i.e., the Jews). The ethnic realities of the Thessalonian correspondence as a whole and 1 Thess 2:14–16 in particular are much messier and more nuanced than that!

RACE AND NATIONALISM: ON SAYING AND HEARING HARD THINGS

Our discussion up to this point should suffice to show that 1 Thessalonians at least, and maybe even Pauline Christianity as a whole, is indistinguishable from the racial and ethnic questions of the first century. The Western world of the twenty-first century is at least as burdened by racial challenges as was the Roman world.¹³ Unfortunately, the church is often the site of racial discord rather than a catalyst for healing, reconciliation, and unity-amidst-difference.¹⁴ In the closing paragraphs of this chapter, I want to consider the relevance of the Thessalonian correspondence and of Pauline Christianity more generally for questions of race, ethnicity, and nationalism.

In the United States, issues of race and/or nationalism are too-often framed as Black and White issues. "Nationalism" is often "White nationalism," whether explicitly or implicitly; conversely, adjectives like *racial* or *ethnic* often connote "African," "African American," and/or "Black." The history of European colonialism and the trans-Atlantic slave trade explains the salience of Black and White relations in American politics and culture. Nevertheless, other racial and/or ethnic groups make up part of the American experience of race-relations. My name and physical appearance identify me as a Latino or Hispanic American, though I also have Asian (Japanese) and White ancestry and upbringing. In contemporary American political discourse, Hispanic identity is associated with immigration issues more often than racial issues. Latinos and Asians are mapped onto a spectrum ranging from White to Black, with some Latinos and/or Asians being "White adjacent" (non-White persons who benefit from or enjoy White privilege),¹⁵ while others are included among "Black and Brown people" or "Black, Indigenous, and People of Color (BIPOC)." It should trouble those of us interested in racial reconciliation that the difference between a "White adjacent" Latino or Asian and a "BIPOC" Latino or Asian is the ideology of the person

---

13. For an important recent discussion of the American context, see Gorman et al., eds., *Slavery's Long Shadow*.

14. See chapter 7.

15. Saad, *Me and White Supremacy*, 15–16.

being categorized. We should be wary of using ethnic or racial labels to police the beliefs and perspectives of the human beings who inhabit "the Black and Brown bodies" we claim to advocate for.

This Black-White spectrum flattens the complexity of race-relations in societies as large and diverse as modern Western societies. Black-White issues, including the history and legacy of slavery, absolutely deserve our attention, but they are not helpful lenses for understanding the experiences of other peoples in the US, including peoples not from western or northern Europe or indigenous Americans.

Also problematic is the tendency to identify features of American culture as "White" and then identify these with oppression, domination, and injustice. In the summer of 2020, amidst the aftermath of George Floyd's murder and the ongoing COVID-19 pandemic, the National Museum of African American History and Culture apologized for and removed its graphic, "Aspects and Assumptions of Whiteness and White Culture in the United States."[16] In this chart on its online Talking about Race portal, "objective, rational linear thinking," a "nuclear family" consisting of "father, mother, and 2.3 children," and a lack of tolerance for deviation from the "single god concept," among other things, were labelled "White." Cause-and-effect relationships, familial bonds, and intolerance for other religious traditions are not natural qualities inherent to any race or ethnicity, nor are they naturally deficient from any race or ethnicity. Applying racial labels to such characteristics or implying that such traits are racially oppressive or unjust neither clarifies nor improves the cause of racial reconciliation.

---

16. Watts, "Smithsonian Race Guidelines," https://www.newsweek.com/smithsonian-race-guidelines-rational-thinking-hard-work-are-white-values-1518333, accessed June 2, 2023.

But perhaps Paul shows us a more excellent way. Our Jewish authors and their Thessalonian readers belong to different "narratives of belonging"—different from each other and different from us. Paul is a descendant of Abraham, "of the race of Israel, the tribe of Benjamin, a Hebrew born from Hebrews" (Phil 3:5). He tells Peter, "we are Jews by birth," and he differentiates them from "gentile sinners" (Gal 2:15). As we saw above, Paul brings this stereotypical way of thinking about non-Jews also to 1 Thessalonians, where he denigrates "the gentiles who do not know God" and their "lustful passion" (1 Thess 4:5). Presumably, comments like these would not bring Paul and his non-Jewish readers together.

Despite their different "narratives of belonging," Paul and his companions nevertheless open themselves to identifying with, embracing, and accepting their readers. As we will see in the next chapter, our authors present themselves as both a nursing mother and a guiding father (1 Thess 2:7, 11–12), grateful for their faithful children who are walking the same path as their parents (2:13–14). For many people, "family" is their first narrative of belonging and, as we saw, the root of the word, *nation*. In two of his more famous letters, Paul uses the metaphor of *adoption* to describe the relationship between his gentile readers and his nation's God (see Gal 4:5; Rom 8:15). To be sure, *adoption* belongs to Jews like Paul (see Rom 9:4). But Paul can say to his gentile readers that they, too, are "children" and "heirs" (Gal 4:7), even "coheirs with Christ" (Rom 8:17).

Paul's openness to his gentile readers is not quite the openness to others that we espouse in our own cultural environment. Paul does not embrace his pagan readers *as pagans* (that is, as devotees of non-Jewish gods). He embraces them as ex-pagan converts to Israel's God, as people who had once "exchanged the glory of the immortal God for the likeness of an image of a mortal human being or birds or animals or reptiles," worshipping "what was created rather than the Creator" (Rom 1:23, 25), but have now "turned to God from idols to serve the living and true God" (1 Thess 1:9). Paul was not a religious pluralist. But he *was* an ethnic pluralist, and in his later letters we find him vehemently rejecting the idea that non-Jewish followers of Jesus should act like or pretend to be Jews. Paul expected his readers to remain gentiles, or, as Paula Fredriksen calls them, "ex-pagan pagans" (that is, non-Jews who have not become Jews but who no longer worship non-Jewish gods).[17]

Perhaps we can find in Paul a model of openness to others *as others*.[18] Paul does not expect or require his readers to become just like him. At the same time, he does not shy away from critiquing weaknesses or failures in his readers' cultures and religions and advocating Jewish culture and religion as a better option for his non-Jewish readers. While we cannot know the details of his interactions with people very different from him, he was apparently friendly enough that he was able to convince non-Jews of the truth and wisdom of his Jewish message. His letters show that he could be passionate, aggressive, even sarcastic. But at its most fundamental level, the story of Paul is one of successful, interethnic engagement with non-Jewish others. Paul's example invites us to practice saying hard things to people who are different from us. But saying hard things *to* others also requires us to be willing to hear hard things *from* others.

In the end, relating to and learning from others who are not like us was always going to be difficult. Even relating to and learning from others who are the most like us is difficult, as anyone with a family can attest. Families are both a

17. Fredriksen, "What Does It Mean," 375n43.
18. Again, see chapter 7.

gift and a burden. We will see Paul and his companions address both of these aspects of family life in the next chapter.

DISCUSSION QUESTIONS

1. How do racial identities, as "narratives of belonging," draw you closer to people you perceive as "like you" and/or separate you from people you perceive as "different from you"?
2. What, if anything, would you change about how you relate to others, both those who share your national, ethnic, or racial identity/-ies and those who do not?
3. Do you have regular, meaningful interaction with people whose "narratives of belonging" differ significantly from your own?
4. What difference does it make, if any, to highlight the persistently ethnic identity of Paul's God as "the Jewish God" or "the God of Israel"? Does this affect your understanding of modern Christianity as a nearly exclusively non-Jewish religion?
5. What is valuable to you about the universal human experience shared by most, if not all, human cultures?
6. What is valuable to you about the particular experiences of distinct national, ethnic, or racial groups?

3

FAMILY

The Gift and Burden of Belonging to Each Other

According to the State of Oklahoma's Seventh Judicial District Court, Kris Williams was not her son's mother. According to the Court's "Findings of Fact," she was listed on her son's birth certificate as "Second Mother," and her son was given her last name.[1] Williams and her son's biological mother were married early in June 2019, and the baby was born in August 2019. Late in November 2021 (shortly after her son's second birthday), Williams's wife and son moved in with the boy's biological father, whom the child knew as "dad," and early the next month her wife received an Emergency Order of Protection from Williams and filed for divorce. There were two women listed on her son's birth certificate as "mother," and presumably during the

1. The District Court's ruling in the case, "Wilson v. Williams," is available online at https://s3.documentcloud.org/documents/23649403/1053622896-20230214-105340-1.pdf, accessed June 12, 2023.

twenty-seven months between his birth and his mothers' divorce he called both women "mom." There was also a man whom the boy knew as "dad" despite not being listed on the boy's birth certificate. No one disputed the child's paternity.

In this chapter, I am not looking to raise questions about the morality or politics or theology of same-sex marriage. In this chapter, I want to consider the tricky dynamics of *family*: what it is, *who* it is, and how we relate to it. Kris Williams's case is interesting because it shows us how differently the term *family* can function in everyday life versus in court, in popular culture versus in technical contexts like law, philosophy, and theology. Those different functions can be very consequential for real, flesh-and-blood people. Some of us will look at Williams's case and see an injustice at a woman denied access to her son and all the rights a mother usually enjoys. Others of us will see a heartbreaking example of what happens when traditional institutions undergo tectonic changes too quickly. No matter what we see in Williams's case, few people would deny that families have immense power, whether to help their members flourish or to scar them. Families, whether factual or fictive (we will define these terms shortly), provide many of us our first and most enduring relationships, for good or for ill. Perhaps the Thessalonian letters speak into some of the complicated questions facing twenty-first-century families.

WHAT IS A FAMILY, AND WHAT IS A FAMILY FOR?

The word *family* has an interesting history. It derives from the Latin word *familia*, which itself derives from the word *famulus*, "slave, servant." The word *familia*, then, referred to the slaves or servants who were part of a household; it only rarely referred to "parents with their children." The normal Latin word for *family* was *domus*, "house," from which we get English words like *domicile* and *domestic*. Notice the irony: English takes a Latin word for "servant, slave" and gets its primary word for the household unit (*familia* → *family*); meanwhile, it takes a Latin word for "household, family" and gets a term for household servant, employee, or slave (*domus* → *domestic*).

Etymology (the study of a word's origins and the evolution of its meaning) does not really offer us much help when trying to understand something as complex as the family, whether in antiquity or today. Our very real experiences with flesh-and-blood families and our very real convictions about ideal families (or about the ideal Family) affect our thoughts and feelings on myriad other controversial questions, from the definition of marriage, regulations affecting public education, and appropriate healthcare policy, to care for the elderly, creating fair and equitable employment systems, and even the structure of the tax code. When we talk about family, we are talking about *everything*, and this can make things messy.

Perhaps we can start at the beginning. At *our* beginning. At birth. Because whatever else a family is, families create, care for, and nurture children. (Not that children are essential for a social unit to be legitimately considered a *family*; rather, the point is that *families* are essential for nurturing and socializing children.) It is a fact of biology that human beings are born too early, before we are ready to do even the most basic things, like support the weight of our own bodies or avoid predators. Horse foals are able to stand, even to run shortly after birth. If human babies were required to do the same to survive, we would all die very young and very alone. Unlike horses and many other mammalian species, we humans are born well before we have any business being on our own. In this sense, families are an extension of the uterus, protecting and providing for the development of human organisms until we are able to move ourselves, feed ourselves, respond to danger for ourselves, and file our own taxes.

In terms of evolutionary biology, then, families are *biological* necessities that enable babies to focus on breathing, eating, pooping, and growing until they can take on some of life's more complicated functions. Perhaps this explains the tendency, especially among northern European and American cultures, to emphasize the so-called "nuclear family" (a pair of adults and their children, though for our purposes we do not need to exclude single-parent families and/or families that include adopted or stepchildren): before it is emotionally or socially or culturally necessary, the family is *biologically* necessary for children to survive into maturity. This biological necessity at least partly explains why families accrue to themselves emotional, social, and cultural significance. A society that does not forge social and cultural institutions to reward robust familial support and sanctions to punish familial neglect will undermine its own survival.

But families do much more than simply provide for babies' physical survival. Under normal circumstances, parents and children experience intense forces of attraction and bonding during mundane actions like breastfeeding, making and maintaining eye-contact, communicating verbally and nonverbally, and so on. Hormones and neurotransmitters are certainly involved in the creation and perception of this attraction, but most of us sense intuitively that a mother's bond with her child is the result of more than simply increased levels of oxytocin. Moreover, these bonds are not restricted to a biological mother and her child. Fathers, grandparents, siblings, and others experience a sense of bonding during the normal activities that make up raising children to maturity, including physical contact, play, reading together, and meeting basic physical needs. In other words, families do not exist simply to meet the needs of helpless infants and hapless children; they also provide intense and intensely personal benefits for those who bear the costs and meet the demands of being a family. Families—not simply blood-relatives, but anyone who performs the *role* of a family member—have transformative effects even on members who are otherwise perfectly capable of providing for their own survival (and filing their own taxes).

Our familial bonds strengthen and lengthen as we develop from infancy through childhood and adolescence and on to adulthood. They strengthen as we learn to reciprocate the emotions and behaviors first exhibited toward us as infants. They lengthen in that strong familial bonds provide safety for children to begin to wander further and further away from familiar environments and the people populating those environments.

In post-industrial societies, characterized by rapid travel, increased mobility, and instant communication, we are exposed to a broader range of people than are our pre-industrial, traditional, and/or agrarian counterparts. This broader exposure has had significant consequences for our experiences with and definitions of family. As more and more of us spend more and more of our regular lives living further away from our immediate and nuclear families, we find others to fulfill the roles usually played by family members. We might not be surprised, then, that as our experience of family broadens to include more people, our definition of *family* similarly expands to include different configurations of people. Society has always had to incorporate variations on the two-parents-with-children model of family, including two adults with no children (whether by choice or infertility), a single parent with children, families with stepchildren, and so on. Polygamous families are

Family

also well-known, in some contemporary cultures but especially historically. In the twenty-first century we are seeing increased acceptance of same-sex family structures. The word *family* increasingly includes voluntary relationships between adults, and the idea of *family* is less and less associated with the creation and raising of children.

However we define the word, *family* is another "narrative of belonging," like race and ethnicity.[2] Families are *imagined communities*, not in the sense that they aren't real, but in the sense that they exist in our heads and are reinforced by the stories we tell and the rhythms of our daily lives. I spent my childhood visiting my dad's parents for Thanksgiving, but my grandparents and I did not share a single gene or chromosome. The man I call "dad" is my stepfather, but I do not call him that. He has been my father since I was four years old, and neither he nor his family treat me as a stepchild. The narrative of belonging we tell of each other does not include the word "step," DNA notwithstanding. And I am not unusual in this regard. Many people live in similar family situations, bonded by stories of belonging even in the absence of shared blood. And even when blood is shared, the blood itself is insufficient for forging the connections that bind one person to another. The stories of belonging we tell ourselves are the difference between a father and a sperm donor, a sibling and a stranger.

FAMILIES—FACTUAL, FICTIVE, BOTH

The early Christians were well known for their use of family language to refer to each other. The New Testament uses the Greek word for "brother" or "sibling," *adelphos* (as in, Phila*delph*ia, "the City of Brotherly Love"), over three hundred times.[3] Sometimes *adelphos* refers to someone's biologi-

2. See the previous chapter.
3. The word *adelphē*, "sister," is used twenty-six times, often to

cal siblings, as in Mark 1:16, when Jesus sees "Simon and Andrew, Simon's *adelphos*." This fairly straightforward use of the word is part of what we are calling a "factual family," that is, someone's actual family, either by birth, adoption, or marriage. I have already referred to my dad, who married my mother when I was four years old; both he and my biological father are part of my "factual family," as are my mothers (by birth and by marriage), my siblings (none of whom issue from both of my biological parents), and my grandparents, aunts, uncles, cousins, and so on.

Much more often, however, the New Testament uses *adelphos* to refer to people who are not "factual family." Among the more striking examples of this is Paul addressing Christians in Rome as his siblings. It starts right at the beginning of the letter: "I do not want you to be unaware, brothers and sisters (*adelphos*), how I often intended to come to you—though I have been prevented from doing so until now—so that I might have some fruit even among you, just as I have also among the rest of the gentiles" (Rom 1:13). It continues right up to the end of the letter: "I urge you, brothers and sisters (*adelphos*), to look out for those who stir up dissensions and intrigues contrary to the teaching that you learned. Stay away from them" (16:17). The Christians in Rome are, in some sense, Paul's family, *even though he has never met them*! Obviously, then, they are not Paul's "factual family."

So what should we call this kind of family? Anthropologists use the term *fictive family* to refer to family-like social bonds that are not based on blood, adoption, or marriage. Sometimes the term *fictive family* is contrasted with *real family*, but this implies that fictive familial bonds are less real or not real, at least not like relations by blood or

---

refer to an actual female sibling or in the phrase "brother(s) and sister(s)."

marriage. Many of us with close relations with "step" family members and/or with strained or broken relations with "real" family members, however, know from experience how people who were not formerly family to us can become family, and, sadly, how family members can become as strangers.

Somewhat scandalously, Jesus was remembered as elevating fictive over factual family bonds when his mother and siblings tried to apprehend him, perhaps for his own good. When someone told him his family were looking for him, he replied, "'Who is my mother, or my siblings?' Then, as he surveyed those sitting around him, he says, 'Behold, my mother and my siblings, for anyone who does the will of God, this is my brother and my sister and my mother'" (Mark 3:33–35). It would be a gross misinterpretation of Jesus' words here if we insisted that his factual mother and siblings were his "real family," while "anyone who does the will of God" is *merely* his "fictive family."

Even people related by birth or by law have to tell themselves stories of mutual belonging to nurture and sustain familial bonds. A blood-relation without any bonding narrative is meaningless; a marriage without any sense of belonging is loveless. So we will not refer to "real families" as if fictive families aren't real and factual families are. Even so, the distinction between familial bonds between family members and familial bonds between people who are not family by blood, adoption, or marriage is useful, so we will use the terms *factual* and *fictive families*, respectively, to refer to these kinds of social relations.

Before we turn to the Thessalonian letters, we should make one more point about how Paul uses the word *siblings* in Romans. As we saw, Paul refers to his readers as his siblings even though he has never met them. This is not just affected rhetoric that tries to schmooze his readers, as if Paul were a used-car salesman trying to close a deal. Paul's message is one of adoption, of forging sibling bonds between peoples who were formerly distant, even at enmity. In perhaps the most famous chapter of perhaps his most famous letter, Paul tells his readers, "You did not receive a spirit of slavery again, which leads to fear; instead, you received a Spirit of adoption, by which we cry out, 'Abba! Father!'" (Rom 8:15). I love the weird grammar of this sentence. Paul starts out using second-person verbs: *you* did not receive a spirit a slavery; *you* received a Spirit of adoption. Second-person verbs differentiate the speaker from the addressee: the readers are separate from the speaker; the readers-as-distinct-from-the-writer have received a Spirit of adoption and not a spirit of slavery. But then, once he tells his reader that they (as distinct from him) have received a Spirit of adoption, *Paul immediately switches from second- to first-person verbs*: "by which *we* cry out, 'Abba! Father!'" With first-person verbs, both the speaker and the addressee are part of the same group.

Notice what Paul does here: he expresses with his grammar the point he makes with his words.[4] Paul's readers, who once were not part of the family of God, received a "Spirit of adoption," a Spirit who takes outsiders and makes them insiders, who takes strangers and makes them siblings. Once he mentions the Spirit of adoption, Paul only uses first-person verbs and pronouns for the rest of Romans 8. The forging of familial bonds achieved through the Spirit of God is the heart of Paul's "ministry of reconciliation" (2 Cor 5:18–20; see also Rom 5:10–11; 11:15), and that forging is reflected in his grammar, which no longer differentiates the speaker from the addressee after mentioning the Spirit of adoption. Paul's readers, like Paul himself, are "children of God, . . . heirs of God and coheirs with Christ"

4. See Rodríguez, *If You Call Yourself a Jew*, esp. 155–59.

Family

(Rom 8:16–17). They are one family, no longer "us" versus "you"; there is now only "us."[5]

THE MULTI-ETHNIC THESSALONIAN FAMILY

First Thessalonians is not a terribly long letter. The English text is about two thousand words, as we mentioned in the chapter 1; the Greek text is even shorter, with fewer than fifteen hundred words. Despite its brevity, Paul and his co-authors use the word *adelphos* (remember: "sibling, brother") nineteen times. Nearly each time the authors are directly addressing their readers. For example, they write, "As you are well aware, brothers and sisters (*adelphos*), the welcome we received from you was not empty" (1 Thess 2:1). The authors do this fourteen times. The other five times they use *adelphos*, it refers to other Christians, whether Timothy (3:2), a hypothetical Christian (4:6), and other Christians in northern and southern Greece (4:10) or in the vicinity of Thessalonica (5:26–27). We find a similar pattern for *adelphos* in 2 Thessalonians.[6] In the Thessalonian letters, the authors use the word for *siblings* or *brothers and sisters* to forge fictive familial bonds between themselves and their readers.

Those of us who are aware of or even used to Christians referring to each other as "brother" or "sister" will not find any of this particularly strange or exotic. It may not even be all that interesting. Perhaps, however, if we are not interested in or surprised by the authors' references to their readers as members of their family, we have failed to

---

5. We can see similar ideas in Galatians 3–4, as well as in Ephesians 3–4.

6. *Adelphos* appears nine times in 2 Thessalonians, seven times to address the readers (2 Thess 1:3; 2:1, 13, 15; 3:1, 6, 13), once to refer to a hypothetical—and wayward—Christian (3:6), and once to reframe the readers' perception of an enemy (3:15).

read these letters well. Part of the problem has been in our use of the word "Christian" to refer to Paul, his co-authors, and their readers. When we call these people "Christian," we risk imposing our own "narrative of belonging" to them and identifying them as characters in a single, unified story: they belong together as members of a single tribe or family, the tribe (or family) of *Christians*.

Unlike us, Paul *never* uses the word *Christian*. The word is rare in the New Testament. The author of Luke-Acts uses it twice, once to explain that Jesus' followers were first called "Christians" in Antioch (Acts 11:26), and once in an outburst by the Jewish King, Agrippa II, who exclaims to Paul, "Are you so quickly persuading me to become a Christian?" (26:28). The author of 1 Peter uses *Christian* as a criminal or judicial accusation and basis for punishment (1 Pet 4:16). But Paul never uses the word in his letters. As far as we can tell, Paul never called anyone a Christian, and his "narratives of belonging" did not include characters he identified as "Christians."

In recent years, scholarship on Paul and his letters has begun to emphasize that Paul's "narrative of belonging" focused on traditional stories of descent from Abraham.[7] According to these scholars, Paul did not divide the world into "Christian vs. non-Christian"; instead, he divided the world into "Jew vs. non-Jew" (or "Jew vs. gentile").[8] When someone views the world this way, Jews are not non-Jews and non-Jews are not Jews. We can see traces of this way of thinking in some of Paul's other letters. For example, Paul declares to the Galatians that he and the leaders of the early Christian movement in Jerusalem agreed that he would take the gospel to "the uncircumcised" (literally, "the

---

7. Fredriksen, *Paul*. See also Hodge, *If Sons, Then Heirs*; Buell, *Why This New Race*.

8. Thiessen, "Construction of Gentiles," 14.

foreskinned"; that is, non-Jews), while Peter and James and John would focus on "the circumcised" (that is, the Jews; see Gal 2:7–9). Later in the same letter, Paul tells Peter, "We are Jews by nature and not gentile sinners" (2:15). In his letter to the Romans, he calls descendants of Abraham's grandson Jacob (also called Israel) "my brothers and sisters (*adelphos*), my kin [or family] according to the flesh" (Rom 9:3), which clearly implies that Jews are related to Paul in a way that non-Jews are not. Jews are Paul's family; non-Jews are not.

This might seem obvious, but it becomes especially interesting when we remember 1 Thessalonians was written to non-Jews in Thessalonica who have turned from worshiping foreign gods embodied in graven images and have committed themselves to worship "the true and living God" of Israel, including his anointed king, Jesus (1 Thess 1:9–10). Paul and Silvanus and Timothy, then, are writing to people who are not their factual family and who are not even their fictive family (at least, in the sense that the nation of Israel, as the descendants of Abraham, are a fictive family). Even so, they address them *as if* their readers are family. In other words, Paul and Silvanus and Timothy have opened themselves to outsiders and are bringing them into their own narrative of belonging. That narrative, however, does not begin with Jesus; it begins with the Creator God, exalted above all that is, who called one man—Abraham—and promised through him to bless all the families of the earth (Gen 12:3). The story might not *begin* with Jesus, but for Paul Jesus is the means by which these outsiders have been adopted and brought into the family. And as we will see in a later chapter, Jesus is the climactic object of both the authors' and the readers' hopes.[9]

---

9. See chapter 5.

All of this would be significant enough if it were all there was. If the Jewish Paul's embrace of his non-Jewish readers were all we could talk about, the Thessalonian letters would be significant for thinking about family, in both the first and the twenty-first centuries. Paul and his companions, however, use three additional metaphors that deepen the relation between Paul, the Thessalonians, and the God of Israel. The first is also the most familiar: The God of Israel is "Father" (Greek: *patēr*). He is not, however, simply "*the* Father," or even "Jesus' Father." He is, repeatedly, "*our* Father." "We thank God always for all of you when we make mention of you in our prayers, ceaselessly remembering the work of your faith, the labor of your love, and the endurance of your hope in our Lord Jesus Christ, in the presence of our God and Father," our authors say at the opening of the letter (1 Thess 1:2–3). Two chapters later, we find a brief prayer that refers twice to "our God and Father" (3:11–13). If Paul, Silvanus, and Timothy are using familial language to expand their fictive family and draw in non-Jews who were, before the gospel, pagans and outsiders, that family is defined not by Paul or Silvanus or Timothy but by the God of Abraham, of Isaac, of Israel.

We cannot emphasize this enough: when our authors mention "God" (Greek: *theos*), they are not talking about a universal, non-ethnic or pan-ethnic deity who is worshiped by and belongs to all nations. The "living and true God" mentioned in 1 Thess 1:9 is the *Jewish* God, and embracing him as Father entails closing the book on pagan narratives of belonging and locating oneself in the Jewish familial narrative. Though Paul does not use the word *adoption* in 1 Thessalonians, the adoption narrative we saw in Romans 8 is implicit in and evoked by the references to Israel's God as "our Father."

Family

A second familial metaphor: Paul and his companions also became like a father to the Thessalonians:

> For you remember, brothers and sisters, our labor and toil: night and day we were at work so that we would not be of any burden for you; we proclaimed to you the gospel of God. You are witnesses—as is God—how devoutly and justly and blamelessly we were among you who believed, as you well know. We became for each one of you like a father toward his own children, encouraging you, consoling you, imploring you to walk in a manner worthy of the God who calls you into his own kingdom and glory. (1 Thess 2:9–12)

Our authors are not just siblings alongside their (younger) Thessalonian brothers and sisters. They also take responsibility for the *paideia*—the "instruction," the "training," the "discipline"—of their new family members, like a father who provides an example for how his children ought to live and guides them on that path. They praise their readers for imitating Paul, Silvanus, and Timothy, their "fathers" in their new family of God (1 Thess 1:6; 2:14).

Third—and this might be most surprising, or at least the most counterintuitive—our authors portray themselves as a nursing mother![10] Immediately prior to likening themselves to an instructive father in the passage we just quoted, we read:

> Though we could have spoken with gravitas, as apostles of Christ, we were instead gentle among you, as a nursing mother who cherishes her own children. So as we longed for you, we decided to

---

10. Paul uses this imagery in a number of his letters. The theme of Paul-as-mother has been most thoroughly explored by Gaventa in *Our Mother Saint Paul*.

> share with you not only the gospel of God but even our very lives, because you had become very dear to us. (1 Thess 2:7–8)

There is a question about what our authors wrote in v. 7. Did they write, "we were instead gentle among you," as I have translated, or did they write, "we were instead like infants among you"? The difference in Greek is one letter; the word for *gentle* is *ēpioi*, and the word for *infants* is *nēpioi*. Fortunately, we do not need to decide the issue now. The broader point is that Paul and his companions, called by the Jewish God to take the gospel to non-Jews, could have "spoken with gravitas" (or "thrown their weight around"; the word is related to *barometer*, which measures the pressure—or weight—of the atmosphere). Rather than doing so, they played the part of a nursing mother caring for her own children.

In a later letter, Paul will chastise his readers for not yet being ready to be weaned off the milk he, as their mother, provides: "So then, brothers and sisters, I could not speak to you as spiritual people; I had to address you as people bound to the flesh. As infants in Christ, I gave you milk to drink rather than solid food, for you were not yet able to handle solid food. But now, you are still not able to handle solid food, because you are still bound to the flesh" (1 Cor 3:1–3). Paul's disappointment with the Corinthians is obvious, almost palpable. But not with the Thessalonians; there is no disappointment or rebuke in 1 Thessalonians 2. Our authors refer to their bond with the ex-pagan Thessalonians warmly; they gave their very selves to the Thessalonians in the same way a mother gives herself to and for her children.

With both parental metaphors—the authors as father, and the authors as mother—Paul, Silvanus, and Timothy draw their ex-pagan pagan readers (i.e., gentiles who no longer live as gentiles, including worshiping gentile gods) into their Jewish familial narrative of belonging. These former pagans do not now belong simply to Paul and his companions; neither do they belong simply to Jesus as "the Christ." They belong to (or better: belong *within*) the centuries- and millennia-long story of Abraham's family. The Thessalonians may not be Jews; they are, however, in the Jewish family: children of Israel's apostle to the nations as well as of Israel's God himself.

THE GIFT AND BURDEN OF FAMILY

In *Witness: Lessons from Elie Wiesel's Classroom*, Rabbi Ariel Burger tells the story of a Jesuit student named Philip, incredulous at Elie Wiesel's account of Jews praying defiant prayers wearing contraband tefillin.[11] "How could you do it?" Philip asks Wiesel; "How could you find it in yourself to pray?"[12] Wiesel's answer, powerful as a response, nevertheless accepts the challenge of Philip's questions:

> It is a good question. Every morning in the prayers, we say, "With a great love have You loved us," and I said it there. It's a part of the prayers, after all. But then I thought, *Come on, really? A great love? In Auschwitz? It is impossible.* As I said, we cannot conceive of that place with God or without God. It is impossible to pray. But I did, and I said that prayer, because my father said it, his father, his grandfather. How could I be the last?

---

11. *Tefillin* are boxes containing verses from Torah, which rest upon the forehead and bicep, and straps that are wrapped around the arm during prayers.

12. Burger, *Witness*, 86–87. I am grateful to Caleb Gilmore for bringing this anecdote to my attention.

When I first heard those last six words—in a Christian sermon on the Psalms—I remember losing something of my breath. "How could I be the last?" In my own version of Christianity, each individual and each generation must decide for itself whether it, too, will deny itself, take up its cross, and follow Jesus (see Mark 8:34). Faith is a matter of trust, but it is the result of choice, of decision, of making up one's mind.

"How could I be the last?" may sound like the gritty determination of a mind made up, but that's not how I heard it. I heard it instead as the quiet recognition of and resignation to the gift and burden of belonging to an Other. Wiesel's forefathers had not experienced the unique horrors of Auschwitz. They had no right—so it seems to me—to lay upon their twentieth-century descendants the obligation to pray about God's great love in a literal valley of death. Had they known, perhaps they would not have.

But this is the nature of faith. Not that we know what the future holds, but that we trust, even in the midst of our ignorance. Wiesel's ancestors had chosen this faith, and with each passing generation, their faith accrued to itself new and greater weight. Who wants to be the generation from whose hands that inheritance falls? And so—again, so it seems to me; I cannot pretend to speak for Professor Wiesel—he holds on. He prays. He finds promise for the future in the burden of the past.

We began this chapter with the story of Kris Williams and the tragedy—for it is tragic, even for those of us with traditional views of marriage and sexuality—of a son who loses one of his mothers and a mother who loses a son. The story is heartbreaking; of course it is. Family narratives should bind together, not tear apart. The story of Elie Wiesel, bound by generations of fathers before him, praying in defiance of all that was Auschwitz, shows us the power of families—as narratives of belonging—to empower humanity in the face of inhumanity.

Paul, Silvanus, and Timothy, like Wiesel and his forebears, prayed to the Creator of the Universe. They likely prayed in distinctively Jewish ways (i.e., in Hebrew [or Aramaic], wearing tefillin, covered with a prayer shawl, oriented toward Jerusalem, as their fathers had done, citing Israel's sacred scriptures). They were, after all, Jews, and they prayed to the Jewish God. If the prayers of Paul and his companions were in any significant ways distinct from their fellow Jews, the distinctions would likely center on being offered through or in the name of the Jewish God's Son, Jesus. But there is no reason to suspect that, in the mid-first century CE, faith in Jesus required significant changes to how prayers were offered.

The surprising thing about Paul's and Silvanus's and Timothy's prayers, if we will see it, is the way they also folded in non-family members, non-Jews, ex-pagan pagans who most definitely did *not* belong in Israel's family's narrative of belonging. The Thessalonians had worshiped what were, at best, lower gods and, at worst, false gods. They looked to the creation of human hands for guidance for their hands. And yet, our authors retold their readers' narrative of belonging, now bringing in these gentiles who had ceased to live like pagans. Paul and his companions became like nursing mothers, gentle as they nurtured the Thessalonians into their new-found family. They became like guiding fathers, instructing the Thessalonians and providing for them an example to imitate. And they pointed the Thessalonians to the Father, the Jewish God who had miraculously induced a great nation from Abraham and Sarah. This God—the God of Israel—was now their God. This family—the family of Israel—was now their family. And despite the fact that the

Thessalonians remained not-Jews, this people—the people of Israel—was now their people.

Family and ethnic narratives of belonging are not simply stories we tell ourselves using words. They are also the stories that shape and bring meaning to how we live our lives. Our ethics. Our morality. In a multi-ethnic family, ethics and morality are bound to get a bit complicated. Do the Thessalonian letters have anything to say about that? We will find out in the next chapter.

DISCUSSION QUESTIONS

1. How do the concepts of *factual families* and *fictive families* relate to your experiences of having and being family? Who are you close to? What makes you close to them? Who are you distant from? What makes you distant from them?
2. What role, if any, does family history have in your own experience of faith and doubt? How does your family history motivate or undermine your own faith?
3. What insight do the terms *gift* and *burden* bring to your own family experiences? How is your family a gift? How is your family a burden? How are you a gift? How are you a burden?
4. How can contemporary families follow Paul's lead and retell their family narratives of belonging to include others who might otherwise be excluded?

4

FROM CHARITY TO SEX

Ethics for a Multi-Ethnic Assembly

"THIS IS WHY EVERYONE hates moral philosophy professors."

To be fair, these are *literally* demonic words, spoken by Michael, a demon who constructs serial torture scenarios. But Eleanor, a horrible person in life but who has made noticeable moral gains in the afterlife, agrees.

The moral philosophy professor in question is Chidi Anagonye, and Chidi has just introduced the famous Trolley Problem, a (hopefully hypothetical) scenario in which a person witnesses a runaway trolley headed toward five people working, apparently absent-mindedly, on the tracks.[1] The witness cannot stop the trolley or warn the bystanders, but they can divert the trolley onto another track, on which only one person is working, unawares. The problem, then, is: should the witness save the five bystanders by diverting

---

1. These are characters from NBC's *The Good Place* (2016–20); see "The Trolley Problem" (season 2, episode 6), which first aired on October 19, 2017.

the trolley and killing the person who is not currently in danger? Or should they not act, allowing—but not *causing*—the deaths of five people?[2]

Michael does not want to weigh the different scenarios or explore the nuances of this or similar ethical dilemmas (suppose five people would die unless they received organs from one healthy person; would it be moral to kill the one to save the five?). Michael just wants to know the answer.

"That's what's so *great* about the Trolley Problem is that there is no right answer," Chidi explains.

This is why everyone hates moral philosophy professors.

In the world of thought experiments and ethical dilemmas, philosophers and professors have all the power to manipulate the details. Suppose a large man gets stuck in the mouth of a small cave, trapping his five companions behind him inside the cave. What should his companions do? Suppose the cave is rapidly filling with water, so that waiting is not an option. Suppose his companions have a stick of dynamite. Suppose the man is stuck head-first, so that his backside is inside the cave and he, unlike his friends, is not in any danger of drowning. Or suppose he is in the opposite position, so that he will drown along with his friends.[3] Academics can imagine all kinds of just-slightly-different scenarios meant to impale their students on horns of dilemmas. And they do so seemingly without experiencing any of the stakes, as if it were nothing to get a person stuck in the opening of a cave, or to turn him round, first with his head outside the cave, then with it in.

---

2. The "Trolley Problem" was introduced by Philippa Foot ("Problem of Abortion," 5–15). Despite being universally (or at least *nearly* universally) known as the "Trolley Problem" or the "Trolley Dilemma," Foot actually used the word *tram* (see pp. 8–9).

3. Foot, "Problem of Abortion," 7.

Spoiler Alert: No wonder Chidi ended up in the Bad Place.

In real life, in the real world, morals and ethics are not *interesting*; they are *consequential*. In the previous chapter we mentioned the example of Kris Williams and the custody case between Williams, her ex-wife, and the biological father of their son. That court case was obviously and literally consequential, in that the familial bonds linking a young boy with three adults significant in his life were at stake, and the court had to decide what was best for the child and/or what was legal according to the statutes and constitutions of the governments with jurisdiction over the case. It feels grotesque—at least to me—to say that their case is *interesting*, as if it were an abstract scenario like the Trolley Problem or the case of our hapless spelunkers. Human beings are not moral dilemmas.

THE ORIGINS AND SCOPE OF MORALITY

Scholars debate whether our earliest social connections (in other words, our family) are the source of our moral instincts or if those instincts are innate, present at birth. On the one hand, moralities vary widely across cultures, so that what one culture sees not just as preferable but even sacred (e.g., the right to choose one's marriage partner on the basis of love) is not just shunned but even reviled and/or ridiculed in another and its opposite is embraced (e.g., the responsibility of parents to arrange appropriate marriage relations for their children). It is hard to see the variety of ways human cultures care for the dead, provide for the weak, punish wrongdoers, interact with adversaries and competitors, define and relate to the sacred or divine, divide labor, reward virtue, and myriad other things and conclude that morality is innate, encoded in our DNA and simply awaiting the appropriate time to emerge, like wisdom teeth or body hair.

And yet . . . most of us have some sense that right and wrong, or at least certain rights and wrongs, transcend culture and are not subject to social conditioning. Certain moral convictions are intuitive, reactions more than conscious choices or even learned habits. For example, experimental psychologist Paul Bloom offers a scenario in which a group of teenagers slap an elderly woman as she waits at a bus stop and laugh as she falls down. "Unless you are a psychopath, you will feel that the teenagers did something wrong. And it is a certain type of wrong. . . . As a moral violation, it connects to certain emotions and desires." Such moral convictions "have their roots in a gut feeling"; they are not the result of philosophical reflection and reasoning.[4] Bloom's research shows that, in fact, many of our moral foundations are present very shortly after birth, months or even days after birth. They may even be innate, woven into the very being of living organisms (including human beings) and the interactions of those organisms with each other and their environments.[5] Even bacterial life-forms—single-cell organisms without brains, nervous systems, or even cellular nuclei—exhibit social tendencies to reward positive behaviors and punish detrimental behaviors.[6] All of this suggests parts, at least, of our moral or ethical foundations are pre-cultural, pre-social, innate to life itself even before the presence or influence of human culture and society.

---

4. Bloom, *Just Babies*, 9–10, 13.

5. For a discussion of "human universals," traits that come to expression in culturally specific ways but are not themselves the products of peculiar or unique cultures, see Brown, "Human Universals," 47–54. See also Goldberg, *Suicide of the West*, 26–28.

6. Damasio, *Strange Order of Things*.

The origins of our ethics "in the gut," arising—as they so often do—from a feeling rather than sustained contemplation, means that our reactions to strangers are frequently "pre-critical," determined even before we have decided how we think we *ought* to behave toward them.[7] Encountering strangers—people not simply unknown but even very different from ourselves, foreign, *strange* (the root of *stranger*)—provokes visceral feelings, reactions that often if not usually override the intentions of our minds. George Orwell explained "the real secret of class distinctions in the West" with breathtaking, offensive honesty:

> The lower classes smell. And here, obviously, you are at an impassable barrier. . . . [Y]ou cannot have an affection for a man whose breath stinks—habitually stinks, I mean. However well you may wish him, however much you may admire his mind and character, if his breath stinks he is horrible and in your heart of hearts you will hate him.[8]

Orwell is talking about class distinctions, but the same dynamics attend to our preference for familiar (*family*-ar) people and our revulsion at—and simultaneous fascination with—strange or exotic people. Ethical questions are, at a basic level, questions about how we relate to and behave toward others, about our rights and responsibilities vis-à-vis other human beings. We might imagine that morality is about "right vs. wrong," but in a world without any other

---

7. In *The Happiness Hypothesis*, Jonathan Haidt compares rational (or *controlled*) and pre-rational (or *automatic*) cognitive processes to a rider (= controlled) astride an elephant (= automatic). Despite our preferences to imagine the rider in control of the elephant's movements, in actual fact the rider goes where the *elephant* wants!

8. Orwell, *Road to Wigan Pier*, 115–16. For an excellent discussion, see Smith, *Desiring the Kingdom*, 28–31.

people, questions about right or wrong vanish. The problem of ethics is the problem of living in a world inhabited by other people. And we, like Paul and his companions, live in a world with some very strange people.

DOES PAUL EVEN CARE ABOUT ETHICS?

As weird as it may sound, New Testament scholars used to think Paul did not care all that much about ethics. Paul, according to these scholars, was so fixated on the any-day-now return of Jesus that he gave no real thought to how people should live in the meantime. According to New Testament scholar Nijay Gupta, "classic studies of Paul's writings and his theology rarely ever address the area of his ethics. . . . [The question of Paul's ethics] is not really one that generated much discussion before the twentieth century—more specifically, before the 1960s."[9]

Such is no longer the case. No matter which way we ask the question, the answer always comes back the same: Paul cared about how his readers acted. Despite his insistence that no one would be set right before God "on the basis of the works of Torah" (Rom 3:20; other translations say, "by works [or deeds] of the law"), Paul nevertheless thought that one's works mattered and would be rewarded or repaid by God. "God will repay each person," he says, "according to their works. To those who persistently seek the glory and honor and immortality of a good deed, he will repay eternal life. On the other hand, to those who disobey the truth out of selfish ambition and instead are led toward injustice, he will repay wrath and anger" (Rom 2:6–8). Paul confronted one of Jesus' original disciples for that disciple's actions, which Paul thought betrayed the gospel (see Gal 2:11–16). In the undisputed letters of Paul alone we find

9. See Gupta, "Ethics," in DPL^2 279, 280.

over 250 imperative verbs, the vast majority of which are instances of Paul telling his readers to do something or not to do something; for example: "Do not destroy the work of God for the sake of food" (Rom 14:20).[10] In 1 Thessalonians alone we find twenty imperative verbs, all but one of them in the last chapter. Paul clearly expected his readers to live according to a certain moral standard or ethical system, and in every single letter we have from him he makes sure to give his readers some instruction on how they should conduct themselves.

TOWARD A PAULINE ETHIC

Even if it is no longer controversial to assume *that* Paul cared about ethics, how to describe his perspective on ethics remains a matter of debate. Many scholars compare Paul to the moral philosophers of his own day—so, not Chidi Anagonye, but men with names like Epictetus, Musonius Rufus, and Seneca—and find Paul to be engaged in a very similar moral project.[11] We will opt to take a different tack. In previous chapters, we have established that the Thessalonian letters were written by ethnically Jewish authors: Paul, Silvanus, and Timothy. To call them "ethnically Jewish" does not discount that these are also *religiously* Jewish authors; instead, this description is meant to help us remember that our authors are very different from their original readers (remember: ex-pagan pagans, or gentiles who no longer worship the gods of the gentiles) as well as very different from ourselves (Western Christian readers who live

10. For *undisputed* versus *disputed* Pauline letters, see chapter 6.

11. One of the most important scholars on Paul and moral philosophy also wrote a significant commentary on the Thessalonian letters; see Malherbe, *Letters to the Thessalonians*. See also Malherbe's earlier book on Paul in pastoral perspective: *Paul and the Thessalonians*.

in a very different world than the one inhabited by Paul and his companions).

These Jews—both ethnic and religious—were not writing the first documents of a new or emerging religion. They were not proclaiming a new god. They were not reading from new scriptures. They were summoning the nations to turn away from their lifeless, worthless gods (this is how Jews, including Paul, spoke of pagan gods)[12] and worship Israel's God. As Paul and his companions note, the Thessalonians "turned to God from idols to serve the living and true God" (1 Thess 1:9). Notice that the Thessalonians were not formerly godless or irreligious or unspiritual or impious; according to Paul—and the vast majority of Jews in antiquity would agree—the Thessalonians were plenty, but wrongly, religious, serving gods that were neither living nor true.

Remember also what we saw in the previous two chapters: our Jewish authors were retelling their own ethnic and familial "narratives of belonging" to include their readers in those narratives. We described those readers as "ex-pagan pagans."[13] As "ex-pagans," they no longer worshiped the gods other pagans worshiped, and they no longer worshiped like other pagans worshiped. They turned their religious and spiritual energies toward Israel's God. As "pagans" still, they did not become Jews. They retained their identities as Greeks, as Thessalonians, as people distinct from Jews. And yet, we should not miss that—despite their

---

12. There are a number of passages that describe foreign gods as without any power to guide, protect, or save, and/or that contrast these gods with the God of Israel. The ten plagues of the Exodus come to mind (Exodus 7–12); so also does the story of Dagon's statue in 1 Samuel 5. For a striking and extended passage, see Wisdom of Solomon 13–16, which Paul seems to be echoing in Rom 1:18–32.

13. This way of referring to Christian gentiles comes from Fredriksen, *Paul*.

ongoing identity as pagans/gentiles—they are nevertheless brought into the story and the community of Israel; they are written into Israel's "narrative of belonging." In later letters, especially Galatians and Romans, Paul will tell his ex-pagan pagan readers that they, too, are children of Abraham and of Abraham's God. They are not merely outsiders who worship the God of Israel, second-class citizens who, like dogs, eat only crumbs that fall from the table. They are insiders, members of the family sitting at the table alongside the rest of the family.

Pauline ethics begin here. His instructions to his ex-pagan pagan readers are given in the tension of the twin realities that his readers are now devotees of Israel's God and subjects of Jesus, Israel's king, and yet they are not Jews and are not subject to the covenantal commandments given to Jews in Torah. Though they, like Israel, worship YHWH, they do not circumcise their sons, observe the distinctive Jewish diet (called *kashrut*, from the same Hebrew stem as *kosher*), and so on. Sometimes, this tension will create difficulties. For example, if gentiles like the Thessalonians are expected to "have no other gods before me" or not to "make for yourself an idol," should they also "remember the Sabbath day and keep it holy" (Exod 20:3, 4, 8 NRSVue)? Even if they are expected not to undergo circumcision themselves, *can* they? What about children born to ex-pagan followers of Jesus? May non-Jewish families circumcise their sons when they are eight days old? *Should* they? Should they follow the example of Daniel and his friends, who refused their pagan king's meat and wine and ate only vegetables and drank water? Or could/should they continue to eat like gentiles? Could/should they eat *with* pagan gentiles, whose food or wine may have some connection with any of the city's pagan temples?

Perhaps surprisingly, many of these particular issues do not arise in the Thessalonian letters, though they do appear in some of Paul's later letters (especially the Corinthian letters and Romans). There is, however, one aspect of biblical (= Old Testament) ethics we should mention. Torah, roughly synonymous with the covenant between Israel and YHWH, placed a number of requirements on Abraham's descendants. Christians have often portrayed these requirements as onerous or impossible, but Jews did not experience them this way. Even in the New Testament, the expectations of Torah could be summarized in terms of two commandments: "You shall love the Lord your God with your whole heart and with your whole life and with your whole mind and with your whole strength [Deut 6:5]," and "You shall love your neighbor as yourself [Lev 19:18]" (Mark 12:30–31). Though Torah's commandments—including circumcision, but also myriad other commandments, called *mitzvot*—did not apply to non-Jews, the commands to love (or worship) the Lord and to love one's neighbors were universal. Failure to worship God as Creator or to love one's neighbor as the image of the Creator God was often likened to sexual infidelity. Significant examples of this analogy include the prophet Hosea, who was commanded to marry a prostitute ("a wife of prostitution"; Hos 1:2 NRSVue) as an image of YHWH's experience with unfaithful Israel. Perhaps even more striking—if such a thing can be imagined—is the image of Jerusalem as an abandoned-daughter-turned-faithless-wife in Ezekiel 16. Even in the New Testament, where the people of God are more likely to be portrayed as a faithful rather than faithless bride, covenant fidelity is easily and often likened to sexual morality (e.g., Eph 5:25–27; Rev 21:2, 9). We will see this idea in Paul's letters, including 1 Thessalonians: worship appropriate to YHWH's covenant is linked with sexual morality, while illicit worship contrary to YHWH's covenant is linked with sexual immorality and/or dysfunction.

With these ideas in mind, let's look at what Paul says specifically to the Thessalonians.

PAULINE ETHICS IN THESSALONICA

We already noted that Paul uses imperative verbs twenty times in 1 Thessalonians. These are verbs that command or prohibit some behavior, like "*Bring* me a cookie," or "*Do not kill* those five workers on the tracks!" The first imperative occurs in the last verse of chapter 4; the remaining nineteen are found in 1 Thessalonians 5. Not all of these imperatives are ethical instructions; in 1 Thess 5:26, for example, the authors tell their readers, "Greet all the brothers and sisters with a holy kiss." Nevertheless, the last two chapters provide almost the entirety of 1 Thessalonians' moral teachings, while the first three chapters have very little by way of instruction. Sure, we could draw inferences from certain passages; for example, when our authors write, "we were encouraged about you, brothers and sisters, despite all our disappointment and affliction, through your faithfulness, because we now live, if you are standing firm in the Lord" (1 Thess 3:7–8), we could offer some ideas about perseverance through suffering or the priority of faith over immediate experience. But our time is better spent looking at the overtly ethical instructions in the letter, and these are found in the last two chapters.

The fourth chapter begins, "So then, finally, brothers and sisters, we ask you and encourage you in the Lord Jesus, that just as you received from us the way you should walk and please God—as indeed you are already walking—so you would progress even further. For you know what instructions we gave you through the Lord Jesus" (1 Thess

4:1–2). Notice the heavy emphasis on the readers' way of life, their conduct. They ought to walk and are walking in a way pleasing to God. The authors had offered instructions in such things when they were in Thessalonica with their readers.

The next two paragraphs (1 Thess 4:3–12) offer the authors' first ethical exhortation. The first paragraph (vv. 3–8) focuses on sex; the second (vv. 9–12), on love, or what used to be called *charity*. Paul and Silvanus and Timothy offer fairly conventional comments here, inasmuch as worship and sex and charity were often linked together. Perhaps the most well-known connection between these three in any of Paul's letters occurs in Romans 1, where all three activities are warped, turned upside-down, and corrupted. Paul links the revelation of God's wrath against impiety and injustice to the misdirected, disordered pagan worship. "They exchanged the truth of God for a lie," complains Paul, "and they worshipped and ministered to what was created rather than the Creator" (Rom 1:25).

Then, famously, Paul draws the first conclusion: disordered worship leads to disordered sex: "So God handed them over to dishonorable passions, since their females exchanged the natural relation for one contrary to nature, just as the males also abandoned the natural relation with a female. They were inflamed by their lust for one another, males committing this shameless deed with other males, and they received the penalty required by their mutual deception" (1:26–27). This passage is famous—or infamous, depending on your perspective—within the context of contemporary debates about sexuality, sexual orientation, and gender identity. Traditional readers find Paul saying homosexuality is sinful, "dishonorable," "contrary to nature," and worthy of "penalty." Some readers find Paul condemning not "homosexuality" but pederasty, an exploitative relationship involving older, high-status males and young boys as the passive participant. This question is too complex and fraught to attempt to solve here, though it would be appropriate to note (a) twenty-first-century debates about sexuality and same-sex marriage are very different from anything Paul would have encountered in the first century;[14] (b) Romans 1 never mentions adult males nor boys nor power imbalances, so pederasty is not likely to have been his target; and (c) Romans 1 is focused on misdirected, disordered worship and its misdirecting, disordering effects on human ethics. Paul certainly describes first female, then male same-sex sexual activity as a consequence and sign of misdirected, disordered worship, and readers in the twenty-first century will need to wrestle with that description head-on as we engage our own cultural, political, and theological questions.

A very similar way of thinking is at work in 1 Thessalonians 4, where we can infer a connection between worship—or faithfulness to "the living and true God" (1 Thess 1:9)—and sex. We should notice two things. First, the reoriented, rightly restored worship mentioned in 1:9 leads to reoriented, rightly restored sexual ethics in 4:3–8. Despite the relative clarity of these six verses overall, commentators debate the meaning of v. 4. Abraham Malherbe translates v. 4 as, "that each one of you learn how to acquire his own wife." On the other hand, Timothy Brookins translates the same verse, "that each of you learn how to gain mastery over his own body."[15] The word that Malherbe translates as *wife*

---

14. There simply was no such thing as "same-sex marriage" in the Greco-Roman world, where two adults would enter a socially recognized relationship like the husband-wife relationship despite being of the same sex.

15. Malherbe, *Letters to the Thessalonians*, 224, 226–28; Brookins, *Thessalonians*, 84.

and Brookins as *body* is a very general word: *skeuos* (lit., "thing, vessel"), which some commentators even suggest may be a euphemism for male genitalia. My own translation of v. 4—"for each one of you to keep control of your self"—agrees with Brookins but preserves the ambiguity of *skeuos* with the imprecise word *self*.

Whatever our authors are saying in v. 4, the gist of vv. 3–8 is clear enough: the Thessalonians are expected to demonstrate the transformation of their religious orientation (see 1:9) by exhibiting control (or mastery) over their sexual desires and behaviors. This is the opposite of the critique Paul will direct at gentile Christians in Rome. In Romans, pagan idolaters lose all control of themselves and are enslaved to their passions. In 1 Thessalonians, ex-pagan pagans show their proper orientation toward the Creator God of Israel by gaining control over their urges. This, Paul and Silvanus and Timothy explain, is what it means to be holy, to be consecrated, to have received the holy Spirit (vv. 3, 7–8).

Second, sex is linked with broader social ethics, especially—but not only—how the Thessalonians relate to outsiders (i.e., non-Christian Thessalonians). Again, this is parallel to what Paul will write in his later letter to the Romans. We have already seen how he proceeds from misdirected, disordered worship (Rom 1:18–25) to misdirected, disordered desire (1:26–27). From there, Paul argues that disordered worship affects not just sexual desire but also social relations, resulting in all kinds of social dysfunction and breakdown. "Since they did not see fit to acknowledge God, God handed them over to an unfit mind, to do things that are not proper, since they are filled with every injustice: wickedness, greediness, and malice; they are full of envy, murder, strife, treachery, malevolence. They are gossipers, slanderers, haters of God, insolent, arrogant, boasters, innovators of evil, disobedient to their parents, senseless, faithless, heartless, merciless" (1:28–31). In Romans, disordered worship leads to disordered desire, and both lead to social dysfunction.

We can see this same movement (worship → sexual ethic → social ethic) in 1 Thessalonians, but whereas this movement in Romans was negative, in 1 Thessalonians it is positive. Now that ex-pagan pagans in Thessalonica have redirected their worship toward Israel's Creator God, his will for them is, first, holiness in terms of their sexual ethic (1 Thess 4:3–8) and, subsequently, charity (or love; 4:9–12). Paul and his coauthors use the word *philadelphia* in v. 9, which I translated "love for one another." They use the at-least-as-familiar word *agapaō* later in the same verse ("you yourselves have been instructed by God *to love* one another"). Whereas Romans 1 builds up to the vice list we quoted from Rom 1:28–31, the ethic of the Thessalonian readers includes love for each other, living peaceably with others, attending to their own affairs, working with their own hands, and conducting themselves with decency. In other words, the movement in 1 Thessalonians (right worship → consecrated sexuality → positive social function) is the mirror image of the movement in Romans (misdirected worship → disordered sexuality → social dysfunction).

The next two paragraphs (1 Thess 4:13—5:11) address topics related to Jesus' *parousia*, which we will talk about in the next chapter. But questions about the future and last (or final) things also point in a thoroughly ethical direction. First, they offer hope to ex-pagan pagan followers of Jesus. Second, they offer warning to pagan opponents of Jesus' followers. And third, they lead to the conclusion in 5:11, with its two imperative verbs: "Therefore, encourage one another, and build one another up, each one the next one, just as you are already doing."

Apart from the closing, the letter ends with a series of rapid-fire instructions; 1 Thess 5:12–21 contain fifteen of the letter's twenty imperative verbs. These instructions aim at two targets: (a) fostering and encouraging internal social cohesion and unity, and (b) pursuing the well-being of and positive encounters with outsiders.[16] Certain themes in these instructions will continue into Paul's later letters; for example, when our authors urge their readers to "devote yourselves to the needs of the weak" (5:14), we would be excused for hearing also echoes of Paul's later words to the Corinthians: "So beware, lest this right of yours become a stumbling block for those who are weak" (1 Cor 8:9; see also Rom 15:1–6). Two recurring words in Paul's ethical instructions, which appear in 1 Thess 5:12–21 as well as Paul's later letters, are *love* (esp. *agapaō* or *agapē*) and *the good* (*agathon* and/or *kalon*). These two concepts are the lenses through which Paul's ethical vision passes.

THE ETHICS OF A MULTI-ETHNIC ASSEMBLY

We have some pretty thick threads to tie together, and space is already running quite short. We will return to these issues in the final chapter, but for now let's conclude with two basic observations.

First, Paul and Silvanus and Timothy's ethical instructions were based in a thoroughly Jewish cultural context, even as they were given to ex-pagan pagans, gentiles who turned away from non-Jewish gods to worship the Jewish God. Greek and Roman moral philosophy and culture had robust traditions about self-mastery and self-control, about virtue, and about how to relate to others. In other words, Greeks and Romans had clear ideas about ethics. But our (Jewish) authors do not embrace or even co-opt those ideas.

16. See chapter 7.

Instead, they turn their (gentile) readers *away* from pagan culture and religion—these are not easily separated even today; they were even more entangled in antiquity—and anchor their ethical instructions in the reordered, reoriented worship of Israel's Creator God. This is quite unlike our own multicultural, pluralist context, where we are hesitant to advocate our own cultural values at the expense of others. As readers in the twenty-first century, we will need to wrestle with the extent to which the Thessalonian letters challenge us to confront not just our own culture's ethical shortcomings, but also those of other cultures.

Even so, and second, the Thessalonian letters are hardly encouraging to the current situation of the American church amidst a secularizing culture. If, as we have argued, Paul perceives a link between worship, sexual desire, and charity toward (or love for) others, the church's current record of sexual dysfunction and social antagonism does not speak well of our orientation toward proper worship. The church is fractured and fragmented over questions about sexuality and gender even as it fails to confront or correct—or seemingly even to repent of!—its own sexual excesses and abuses. Some of us point to Romans 1 to advance our lines in the culture wars, as if Paul's target were homosexuality rather than sexual dysfunction. Whatever we might think of the wider culture's obsessions with sex and sexual expression, those same obsessions are rampant among those of us whom Paul expects to "keep control of our selves" (1 Thess 4:4). When Paul and his companions write, "God is the avenger of all these things" (4:6), this is a warning for *Christians*, not non-Christians.

Pauline ethics as they appear in the Thessalonian letters are less an encouragement that we, today, are doing well, and more a provocation to examine ourselves more honestly and enact appropriate changes.

The message for us from these letters is simple: we can do better.

DISCUSSION QUESTIONS

1. Is Paul's link between worship, sex, and charity relevant for thinking about ethics today? What does religion or spirituality have to do with desire? How does religion or spirituality lead to enlightened (or depraved) social relations?

2. Are you aware of any instances of sexual excess or abuse within the church, either personally or through stories in the media? How did officials within the church respond? How were their responses indicative of *love (agapē)* or *the good (agathon)*? How were their responses less than *agapē* or *agathon*?

3. Are you aware of any instances, either personally or through stories in the media, of the Christians or the church extending love and/or goodness across lines of difference, even in the face of significant and important disagreement?

4. Assuming we cannot just snap our fingers and make others agree with us, what are actions we can take to foster and encourage dialogue, understanding, and goodwill with other Christians with whom we have significant and important disagreements?

5. Assuming we cannot just snap our fingers and make others like us, what actions can we take to foster and encourage dialogue, understanding, and goodwill with people who disagree with, maybe even dislike, Christianity?

6. What are two or three concrete ways you can bring *love* (*agapē*) and *the good* (*agathon*) to those around you, both within and outside the church?

5

VISIONS OF THE FUTURE

This Ambiguous Thing Called "Eschatology"

"It's difficult to make predictions, especially about the future."

I have always heard this quote attributed to New York Yankees catcher Yogi Berra, though he certainly did not coin this phrase. As I was doing the research for this chapter, however, I couldn't even find evidence that Berra ever said these words, which brings to mind another Yogi-ism: "I really didn't say everything I said."

Wherever it comes from, there seems to be agreement that this is a Danish proverb, first appearing in print in 1948 but reporting something allegedly said in 1937–38.

The English word *eschatology* comes from two Greek stems: *eschaton*, meaning "last or final thing," and *logia*, "word, discourse," or, by extension, "science, theory, doctrine." *Eschatology*, then, is the study or theory or doctrine of last things, or the end of time, or the end of the world. It is fundamentally oriented toward the future, which makes eschatology fundamentally unclear, even unsure, because it's difficult to make predictions, especially about the future.

And yet, the Thessalonian letters have a lot to say about eschatology and the future. And as much as I might want to, we cannot avoid talking about eschatology if we're talking about the Thessalonian letters. So here is my offer: we can read biblical texts about the future, and we can do some serious, careful investigations into those texts, and we can even suggest what we think the authors of those texts expected for the future. But—and this is key—nothing in this chapter is meant as a prediction, especially about the future. After all, Paul himself was not great at those pesky predictions. In his first letter, he seems to expect Jesus to return during his own lifetime. In a passage we will look at more closely later in this chapter, Paul and his companions write, "We who remain alive until the *parousia* of the Lord will in no way precede those who have fallen asleep. The Lord himself—with a command, with the voice of the archangel and the trumpet of God—will descend from heaven, and the dead in Christ will rise up first, and then we who remain alive will be gathered up in the clouds together with them to meet with the Lord in the air" (1 Thess 4:15–17). As I write in 2023, it would seem things didn't turn out as Paul expected. If *the* apostle struggled to understand future events, who am I to tell you about events yet to unfold?

THE INTERSECTION OF THEOLOGY AND THE FUTURE

Even so, we all live under the constant pressure of an uncertain future. And once again, just as with ethnicity and family, the stories—or narratives—we tell ourselves play a large part in how we identify ourselves and others with regard to the future. Some of us have fundamentally optimistic views of the world and its future; we see progress all around us and feel a sense that the world is getting better all the time. This view of the world correlates with a theological view called *postmillennialism*, which is related to a particular scene from the book of Revelation:

> Then I saw an angel coming down from heaven, holding in his hand the key to the bottomless pit and a great chain. He seized the dragon, that ancient serpent, who is the devil and Satan, and bound him for a thousand years. . . . Then I saw thrones, and those seated on them were given authority to judge. I also saw the souls of those who had been beheaded for their testimony to Jesus and for the word of God. They had not worshiped the beast or its image and had not received its brand on their foreheads or their hands. They came to life and reigned with Christ a thousand years. (Rev 20:1–2, 4 NRSVue)

According to postmillennialist views, the gospel will gradually spread and improve the world, eradicating problems like war, poverty, and oppression. The period of this improvement is the thousand-year reign referred to in Rev 20:4, and at the end of this millennial reign (hence, *post*millennialism), Christ will return. Such views were particularly prominent in the nineteenth century and were associated especially with "social gospel" movements that aimed at improving the here-and-now lives of here-and-now people.

Not everyone, of course, shares this optimistic orientation toward the future; some of us—to me, it feels like the majority—have fundamentally pessimistic views of the world and its future. Despite the fact—yes, the *fact*!—that the world is not as bad as most of us think, nor is it getting inexorably worse, many of us tend to see deterioration all around and feel a sense that the world is falling apart, with things only and always getting worse.[1] This view of the world correlates with a theological view called *premillennialism*, with a very different interpretation of the scene from Revelation 20. According to premillennialist views, forces of evil and entropy and decay increasingly corrupt the world, increasing suffering and persecution, especially for anyone who remains faithful to God. The period of this corruption will only come to an end when Christ returns (the first time?) to begin the thousand-year reign referred to in Rev 20:4 (hence, *pre*millennialism). Such views became particularly prominent in the twentieth century, following the horrors of the First World War, and are particularly evident in religious communities that withdraw from what they perceive as a depraved and damned world and have a sense of persecution from malign forces all around.

We should mention one more interpretation of Rev 20:1–6: *amillennialism*. Roughly speaking, this view denies any concrete, literal reality to an actual millennial kingdom (hence, *a*millennialism). After all, Rev 20:1–6 is chock-full of metaphorical and symbolic imagery: a key, a bottomless pit, a great chain, a dragon, and so on. It would be strange indeed if, in the midst of all this non-literal imagery, the thousand-year reign were the one thing that referred to an actual, real thing. While amillennialists (like myself) do not expect an actual thousand-year reign, that does not mean we dismiss the reign of Christ as merely symbolic or metaphorical. We just do not think Revelation 20 is predicting or promising a millennial kingdom. In the spirit of our earlier hesitance to make predictions ("especially about the future"), I will be surprised and open to correction if Christ returns at either the beginning or the end of a millennial rule.

More importantly, amillennialism is not necessarily tied to either an optimistic or pessimistic stance toward

1. See Rosling et al., *Factfulness*.

the future. On the one hand, amillennialists may be either optimistic or pessimistic. Or, on the other hand, amillennialists may resist viewing history as either generally improving or generally decaying. Instead, this world (including all its cultures) is fallen and broken, so we should not be surprised that things like poverty, war, and oppression continue despite efforts at every level of society to improve the lives of suffering people. (Thus, the postmillennialists were perhaps a bit too naïve to imagine that they could eradicate the effects of creation's fallenness and brokenness.) At the same time, this world (including all its cultures) is the expression of God's creative power and the location within which he continues to work, so we should be grateful—and perhaps not surprised—for the social, cultural, political, and technological advances we see in society. (Thus, the premillennialists were perhaps a bit too cynical to imagine the effects of creation's fallenness and brokenness negated its goodness or the impulse of humanity to imitate God by being creative within creation.) We should probably avoid either optimism or pessimism and instead recognize that this good creation is also broken, that this fallen world is also the site of God's restorative and redemptive activity. You know, "for God so loved the world" and all that....

ESCHATOLOGY AND THE END OF HISTORY

Before we turn to the letters to the Thessalonians, we need to place our authors' expectations for the future within the broader historical context of Jewish thinking about the future in the first centuries BCE and CE. And here we need to introduce another easily misunderstood word: *apocalypse*. According to the Cambridge Dictionary, *apocalypse* means "a very serious event resulting in great destruction and change," or "an event resulting in great destruction and violent change."² A quick search on the Internet Movie Database (IMDb) for "apocalypse" returns Francis Ford Coppola's classic, *Apocalypse Now* (1979), or the slightly less venerable *X-Men Apocalypse* (2016), along with a host of other cinematic offerings.³

This is not what *apocalypse* meant in Paul's day.

The word *apocalypse* is just an English version of the Greek word *apokalypsis* (with the emphasis on the third syllable: *a • pah • KAH • leep • sis*), which simply means "uncovering, disclosure, revelation, manifestation." When someone confesses their love for the first time, this is an *apokalypsis*, a revelation. When someone removes their hat or pulls back a veil, this is an *apokalypsis*, an unveiling. Or when a deity discloses some mystery, whether about a complex and chaotic world or about an unknown future, this, too, is an *apokalypsis*. The word does not carry any scary connotations of death or destruction; it is all about making something known. Of course, in an unjust world where justice *will* win out, the *apokalypsis* of God's righteousness, his judgment against oppression and corruption, and his overturning the powers will look an awful lot like death and destruction to an awful lot of people. But to the harried and obstinate faithful, the *apokalypsis* of God's righteousness will look like vindication.

This is both a comfort and a warning.

The adjective *apocalyptic* describes something in terms of an unveiling or a revealing. In ancient Jewish apocalyptic literature, which flourished especially about two hundred years on either side of Paul (c. 200 BCE–200 CE), the thing that was usually revealed was either the hidden structure

---

2. https://dictionary.cambridge.org/dictionary/english/apocalypse, accessed July 15, 2023.

3. https://www.imdb.com/find/?q=apocalypse, accessed July 15, 2023.

of the universe or the as-yet-unfolded events of the future. Often, both structure (= space) and events (= time) are unveiled, as when John sees "a door open to heaven" (or "in the sky") and a voice commanding him to pass through that door. The voice tells him, "I will show you the things that must take place after these things" (= time; Rev 4:1), and then shows him the hidden throne room of God (= space; see Revelation 4–5).

For now, the important thing about apocalyptic is how it works as a worldview, as a way of explaining everyday, normal, taken-for-granted reality. In a world viewed through apocalyptic lenses, both space and time are mysterious, their full reality concealed from human knowledge and reason. Even when God decides to unveil the full reality of space, time, or both, that full reality is overwhelming and incomprehensible to those who see it. A common theme in apocalyptic literature is the presence of an angel or another being who explains to the recipient of God's revelation what they are seeing. For example, a nearby "attendant" explains Daniel's dream to him (Dan 7:16 NRSVue). In the New Testament, an angel explains to John about "the woman" and the seven-headed, ten-horned beast upon which she rides (Rev 14:7). In an apocalyptic perspective, the world is too obscure, even strange to be understood by one's senses. In fact, the eyes and ears can be quite deceptive, unless a person remains faithful to the God who created the cosmos and who rules it despite the apparent strength of his opponents.

This brings us to one last point before we turn to the Thessalonian letters. Very much of Christian eschatology is other-worldly, in that very many Christian ideas about "heaven" or "eternity" imagine that these are places separate or distinct or removed from earth. "Some glad morning when this life is over," goes the popular song, "I'll fly away;

to a home on God's celestial shore, I'll fly away." But here we find a tension in Jewish and early Christian apocalyptic expectations for the cosmos and the future. Yes, many apocalypses involve some kind of "heavenly journey." John, as we saw, sees a door in heaven and is summoned "up here" (Rev 4:1). Elijah, famously, was taken up into heaven in a flaming chariot by a whirlwind (tornado? 2 Kgs 2:11). Jesus tells his disciples he is leaving them to return to the Father, who, presumably, is somewhere else (John 14:28), and another author even describes Jesus leaving earth and ascending into the clouds (Luke 24:51; Acts 1:9). At least part of the reason that heaven is so hidden and obscured must be its distance from earth.

That distance, however, should not obscure from us that *this world* is itself the good work of God's creative impulse. "The heavens are telling the glory of God," says the psalmist, "and the firmament proclaims his handiwork" (Psa 19:1 NRSVue). Paul, in his most well-known letter, explains, "The eager expectation of creation is anticipating the unveiling of the children of God, for creation was subjected to futility—not of its own choosing but because of the one who subjected it—in hope that even creation itself will be set free from the enslavement of decay for the freedom of the glory of the children of God" (Rom 8:19–21). (Notice the word *unveiling*, which is our Greek word, *apokalypsis*.) Jews in antiquity—including the early Christians and the apostle Paul—did not anticipate the destruction of this world and the evacuation of the faithful from this doomed planet to some eternal, spiritual abode. Earth is not (and will not be) Alderaan. Even in the book of Revelation, which contains graphic and catastrophic scenes of destruction and punishment, the earth is not dissolved out of existence. John sees "the new Jerusalem, the holy city, descending out of heaven from God" (Rev 21:2), and an angel takes him up on "a large, high mountain" to look upon the descending city (21:10). Notice the direction of movement: God and his city come down to earth, rather than God, like an alien ship above a Nebraskan cornfield, plucking the elect off the earth and up into heaven. This is even one of the mysteries of the Christian faith: heaven is, somehow and in some sense, *here*; eternity is, somehow and in some sense, *now*.

When, therefore, we speak of "the end of the world" or "the end of history," we should keep in mind that we are speaking at least partly figuratively, metaphorically. To the extent that the cosmos is the site of brokenness, sin, evil, oppression, suffering, and injustice—"subjected," as Paul said, "to futility" (see Rom 8:20)—it will be changed and transformed on the last day (remember: *eschaton* means "last or final"). *This* world, or sometimes the Bible calls it "this age," will come to an end. But *the* world goes on, renewed, restored to its original goodness, as it was "in the beginning" (see Gen 1:1; see also the repetitive use of "good" throughout Genesis 1). "The end" is the end of injustice. The end of brokenness. The end of fallenness. The end of sin, of death, of suffering. It is not the end of the heavens that declare God's majesty, nor of the earth in which he works.

ESCHATOLOGY AND THE THESSALONIAN LETTERS

And so we turn to the Thessalonian correspondence. Considering the relative brevity of 1 Thessalonians (at least when compared to Paul's more famous letters, especially Romans or either of the Corinthian letters), the future-oriented, eschatological sections take up a surprisingly large amount of the letter: the final one-third of chapter 4 and the first half of chapter 5 (1 Thess 4:13—5:11). First Thessalonians 4–5, as we saw, are particularly focused on providing ethical instructions from our Jewish authors to their non-Jewish readers.[4] We should probably remember, then, that the eschatological teachings in these chapters are not primarily instructions regarding what the Thessalonians should *think*; the point of this part of the letter is to remind the Thessalonians how they should *behave*. In other words, eschatology is also about ethics.

We already noted, back in chapter 1, that some form of the phrase "as you well know" occurs nearly ten times in 1 Thessalonians. So it is striking that our section begins with the letter's only note of the readers' potential *ignorance*: "We do not want you to be ignorant, brothers and sisters, about those who have fallen asleep, lest you grieve like those who have no hope" (1 Thess 4:13). The language of "falling asleep," then as now, is a euphemism for death, as is evident from the fact that such falling asleep is likely to provoke grief. In this context, "the rest, who have no hope" likely refers to current pagans, like our readers used to be. Views about death, the possibility of an afterlife, and the continued existence and fate of the soul after death varied among non-Jews. That Paul and Silvanus and Timothy describe gentiles as "having no hope" is polemical and likely to be debated by their contemporaries. Pagans, like Jews, found ways of maintaining hope in the prospect of death. Such ways included the hope of being remembered (especially for an honorable or noble death), or of joining one's ancestors, or of continued existence in some post-mortem state.

Even so, the Thessalonians were apparently agonizing over the fate of their loved ones who had died and so could not live to see Jesus' *parousia* (we will discuss this term shortly). Paul and his companions, then, are not contrasting their Christian hope with the pagans' lack of hope; our authors are contrasting the hope their readers *ought* to

4. See the previous chapter.

have with the current *failure* of their hope. In other words, this is the one place in the letter where there seems to be an implicit critique or correction of the readers:

> If we believe that Jesus died and rose, then we also believe God, through Jesus, will lead those who have fallen asleep along with him. For this is what we said to you by the word of the Lord: We who remain alive until the *parousia* of the Lord will in no way precede those who have fallen asleep. The Lord himself—with a command, with the voice of the archangel and the trumpet of God—will descend from heaven, and the dead in Christ will rise up first, and then we who remain alive will be gathered up in the clouds together with them to meet with the Lord in the air. And so we will always be with the Lord. So then, encourage one another with these words. (1 Thess 4:14–18)

My translation of the beginning of v. 15 conveys a sense of reminder, as if the authors have already said such things to Thessalonians and are now reminding them of what they should already know: "this is what we said to you by the word of the Lord." We should not push the idea of reminder too hard, though; the same phrase could also be translated, "For this is what we are saying to you through the word of the Lord." If this latter translation better conveys the authors' sense, then what follows is new information. I have opted for the first translation because it seems to me that Paul, when he was in Thessalonica, must have taught at least something like v. 14, that God would raise "those who have fallen asleep" in the same way that he raised Jesus.

The rest of the paragraph describes future events, but it does so in ways that are already familiar to the Thessalonians. Paul's description of the events surrounding Jesus' *parousia* mimics the arrival of important visitors to a city and the welcome city leaders would extend to that visitor and their entourage. The word *parousia* means "presence," as opposed to "absence." The anticipated *parousia* of a person who is currently absent gives the word the sense of "arrival" (as in, "the beginning of a now-absent-person's presence"), or "coming" (as in, "the imminent presence of a now-absent person"). In theological discussions, the word *Parousia* (with a capital P) is often used in a technical sense, with the meaning, "Second Coming." According to Abraham Malherbe, *parousia* "was derived from pagan Greek usage, of the ceremonial arrival of a king or ruler with honors or of the coming of a god to help people in need."[5] For example, when Alexander the Great first planned to go to Jerusalem, the Jewish high priest Jaddua was understandably anxious about meeting the leader of the Greek military juggernaut. But after God appeared to Jaddua in a dream and told him not to resist Alexander, the high priest took appropriate action and "awaited the coming (*parousia*) of the king" (Josephus, *Antiquities of the Jews*, 11.328 LCL). As Alexander approaches Jerusalem, Jaddua and the Jews come out meet him and escort him back into the city:

> When he [i.e., Jaddua] learned that Alexander was not far from the city, he went out with the priests and the body of citizens, and ... met him at a certain place called Saphein.... [Alexander] gave his hand to the high priest and, with the Jews running beside him, entered the city. Then he went up to the temple, where he sacrificed to God under the direction of the high priest, and showed due honour to the priests and to the high priest himself. (Josephus, *Antiquities of the Jews*, 13.329, 336–37 LCL)

---

5. Malherbe, *Letters to the Thessalonians*, 272.

A similar scene unfolds at the end of Acts, though this time not for a king. As Paul approached Rome, he and his companions were met on the road and escorted into the city. Luke says, "when the brothers and sisters heard the news about us, they came out as far as the Forum of Appius and the Three Taverns to meet us" (Acts 28:15). The Forum of Appius was forty-three miles south of Rome, while Three Taverns was thirty-three miles from Rome. These distances give us some sense of the importance of greeting important visitors to one's city.

Josephus's description of Jerusalem's reception of Alexander the Great and Acts's description of the Roman Christians' reception of Paul help us see the scene in 1 Thess 4:16–17 differently. Paul and Silvanus and Timothy are not describing the *escape* of Christians *from* earth; they are describing the *return* of Jesus *to* earth. Jesus—"the Lord himself" (4:16)—issues a command, or else the archangel issues the command on Jesus' signal, and "the trumpet of God" heralds his *parousia*, his arrival. The word for trumpet, *salpinx* in Greek, often translates the Hebrew word *shofar*, a horn blown for military and/or religious purposes. (In antiquity, miliary and religious purposes often overlapped.) In Exodus 19, the *shofar* (LXX[6] = *salpinx*) announces YHWH's descent and arrival upon Mt Sinai and summons the people into YHWH's presence.[7] Similarly, in 1 Thessalonians 4, the

---

6. The Roman numeral LXX (= 70) is the standard abbreviation for the Septuagint, the Greek version of the Hebrew Bible/Old Testament that was translated in the second and first centuries BCE. The LXX includes some texts that are not included in many Protestant editions of the Old Testament (nor the Jewish Tanakh), though a number of Christian denominations (e.g., Roman Catholics and Orthodox) consider these texts "deuterocanonical" and part of the Bible. Some of these latter texts were originally composed in Greek (e.g., 2 Maccabees).

7. Exodus 19:13 uses the Hebrew word *yôbēl*, a synonym of *shofar*

sounding of the *salpinx* heralds Jesus' arrival, his *parousia*, and summons believers—the dead first, then also those who remain alive—to meet him as he returns to earth from heaven, "in the clouds" and "in the air," to escort him and his royal entourage ("his holy ones"; see 3:13). Rather than initiating earth's self-destruct sequence, Jesus' *parousia* inaugurates the cohabitation of God and humanity *on earth*, without the presence or threat of death. In other words, 1 Thessalonians 4 reverses the movement of Genesis 3, where death enters creation, humanity is removed from the Garden, and distance begins to separate God from humans.

Now that we have reframed Paul's description of Jesus' *parousia*—not "the beginning of the end of the world," but rather "the renewal of the world"—we are in a good position to notice the most important part of Paul's eschatology. For Paul, eschatology transforms his readers' identity (see chapters 2 and 3, above) and results in a new ethic (see chapter 4, above). As for their identity, they are "children of light" and "children of the day," as opposed to their adversaries, who are, implicitly, "of the night" and "of the darkness" (1 Thess 5:5). As for their ethics, their behavior is alert and sober, as befits the day, rather than languid and inebriated (5:6–8). The description of the ex-pagan gentile believers in Thessalonica bears a striking resemblance to a famous passage from the *Rule of the Community*, a text discovered in 1947 among the Dead Sea Scrolls, near Qumran:

> [God] has created human beings to govern the world, and has appointed for them two spirits in which to walk until the time of his visitation: the spirits of truth and deceit. Those born of truth spring from a fountain of light, but those born of deceit spring from a source of darkness. All the

---

(see Exod 19:16, 19). The LXX uses *salpinx* for both words. See Jones, "Musical Instruments," in *ABD* 4:934–39.

children of righteousness are ruled by the Prince of Light and walk in the ways of light, but all the children of deceit are ruled by the Angel of Darkness and walk in the ways of darkness. . . . But the God of Israel and his Angel of Truth will succor all the children of light. (1QS 3.17–21, 24–25 Vermes [modified])

We should make at least three observations. First, for the author of the *Rule*, two spirits rule over all humanity: a spirit of truth (and light) and a spirit of deceit (and darkness). Second, the spirit of truth (also called the "Prince of Light") rules over the children of light, and the spirit of deceit (also called the "Angel of Darkness") rules over the children of darkness. Third, human behavior is the result of these two spirits; the children of light, governed by the Prince of Light, walk in the light, while the children of darkness, governed by the Angel of darkness, walk in darkness.

First Thessalonians echoes most of these ideas (it does not mention ruling spirits of truth/light and deceit/darkness, though Paul does express similar ideas in some of his other letters). First Thessalonians is surprising in comparison to the *Rule*, however, because the community in the *Rule* drew a sharp line between themselves and gentiles, and they placed Jews who did not observe Torah the way they did on the gentile side of the line. Paul and his companions, in contrast, include former-pagan *gentiles* among the children of light. These gentiles have become children of light "through our Lord Jesus Christ" (1 Thess 5:9). Also, despite the equally bright line Paul and his companions draw between children of the light/day and children of the darkness/night, the ex-pagan followers of Jesus are nevertheless expected to pursue the good (*agathon*), even for people on the other side of that line (1 Thess 5:15; see also 3:12; 4:12).[8]

8. See chapter 7.

Visions of the Future

Before we wrap up our discussion of eschatology, we should consider a paragraph from 2 Thessalonians, where Paul and Silvanus and Timothy refer to an obscure "man of lawlessness," whom they also call "the son of destruction." This man of lawlessness declares "that he himself is a god" (2 Thess 2:4) and is temporarily restrained until it is time for him to be revealed (2:6–8). His arrival—the word is *parousia*, just like with Jesus' arrival—will be accompanied by all manner of signs and wonders, but these will be false signs that deceive anyone who is not anchored to "the love of truth" (2:9–10). The paragraph ends with a hint that God grants unbelievers what they want: they found pleasure in injustice, so he sent "an agent of deception" to give them what they asked for (2:11–12). This passage has generated a lot of discussion among readers with a premillennialist perspective (remember: Jesus returns *before* the millennial kingdom to intervene in a world that otherwise is only getting increasingly depraved). This "man of lawlessness" who sets himself as an object of worship is easily identified with the "Antichrists" mentioned in 1 and 2 John and the Beast mentioned in Revelation and then projected into the future as a sign of the depth of creation's corruption and opposition to God the Father and to Jesus.

What exactly Paul and Silvanus and Timothy meant or who they are referring to—or even if Paul and Silvanus and Timothy actually wrote these words (see the next chapter)—is beyond our ability to determine. Augustine, the famous North African bishop of Hippo, acknowledges he does not know what the Thessalonians knew and so is unable to provide the crucial context for interpreting the enigmatic words of 2 Thessalonians 2. "I admit that I am completely at a loss as to his meaning," Augustine begrudgingly admits (*Civ.*, 20.19 LCL). If Augustine was not able to figure out the apostle's meaning, perhaps we should maintain a posture of humility regarding our own ability to interpret this passage.

My hunch, though, is that Paul was not talking about people or events in the twenty-first century or later. Perhaps he was talking about people or events from his own time. Just ten years before Paul's first visit to Thessalonica, Emperor Gaius (also known as Caligula, which means "Little Boot") planned to install a statue of himself in the Jerusalem temple; only his assassination in 41 CE prevented this act of desecration that surely would have led to war a quarter-century earlier than the actual war between Jews and Romans in 66 CE. Although Caligula was already dead and gone by the time 2 Thessalonians was written, Paul and his co-authors may have expected a future Roman emperor to succeed where Caligula had come up short. Such an expectation may have found support in Israel's prophetic tradition, such as Daniel's "desolating sacrilege" (Dan 9:27; 11:31; 12:11 NRSVue), and perhaps in the teaching of Jesus (e.g., Mark 13:14–23). Alternatively, perhaps Paul and his companions were talking about *kinds* of people, with "man of lawlessness" describing a *type* of figure rather than a specific individual. Either way, we should notice the actual guarantee of God's work in the world: not miracles, not signs, not wonders that impress crowds. What marks out "those who are being destroyed" is their failure to "accept the love of truth, in which case they would be saved" (2:10). Even in the face of eschatological ambiguity, when we hesitate to make predictions—especially about the future!—we can be confident that the practice of love (*agapaō/agapē*) and seeking the good (*agathon*) will keep us steadfast until the day of the Lord actually comes.

THE FUTURE OF THE TWENTY-FIRST CENTURY

So what about us? What about *our* future? The future is no less uncertain today than it was in the first century. Maybe we are less worried than were Paul and his companions about a man (or men) of lawlessness, the work of Satan (or the satan) in frustrating our plans, or the effect of false miracles and wonders in ginning up the ire of urban mobs, but then again, maybe we're not. Not that long ago the United States was inflamed by public protests and violence as racial tensions were agitated and added to the tensions of a global pandemic, and those protests extended even to other countries. Just months later, the tradition of peaceful transfer of power was disrupted as political tensions were agitated amidst fears and conspiracies about electoral integrity and fraud. Today, questions concerning inflation, immigration, spending policy, interest rates, energy and housing costs, climate and natural disasters, wars both actual and potential, and myriad other issues make the future unpredictable, even scary. Demagogues on the Left and the Right make urban mobs (or, if we prefer less fraught language, public demonstrations) a near-constant reality.

In light of all this uncertainty, should we plan for the future and/or retirement? If so, do we invest in public markets or real estate, or should we horde cash in our mattresses? Can or ought we rely on public institutions like Social Security or National Insurance for our future? Can we count on electoral systems to measure accurately the will of the voting public and ensure the stability and viability of democratic-republican government? Should we stockpile food and ammunition for the always-just-over-the-horizon collapse of civilization, or should we lean into an enduringly robust social fabric and trust each other to maintain systems of commerce, communication, and other forms of social interaction? Is it worth having children in today's world? Is the expanse between racial groups so vast that we will never be able to forge a truly multi-ethnic, pluralist society with room for different peoples living differently but still together? Is our future *Star Trek*, where problems like scarcity and war between humans have seemingly been resolved, freeing us up for exploration and conflict on new frontiers? Or is our future *Hunger Games*, where dystopian forces conspire to screw us all, either as tribute for lethal entertainment or as numbed spectators enjoying the suffering of fellow human beings?

Perhaps we ought to develop amillennialist instincts that resist both the optimistic vision of the-future-as-*Star-Trek* and the pessimistic vision of the-future-as-*Hunger-Games*. Perhaps the world in ten, fifty, a hundred, or even five hundred years will be a lot like it is now and was ten, fifty, a hundred, even five hundred years ago: fraught with the consequences of human brokenness and injustice *and also* populated by human beings working to nurture wholeness and justice. I am reminded of a colleague, a grown, fully mature human being with doctoral qualifications, who grudgingly admits he finds himself quoting Disney's *Frozen II* more often than he'd like: "Just do the next right thing; take a step, step again. It is all that I came to do: the next right thing."

In the end, eschatology may be less about ideas concerning the future and more about our behavior in the present.[9] Paul and Silvanus and Timothy don't *not* sound like Anna ("Just do the next right thing"): "We are neither of the night nor of the darkness. Therefore, we do not sleep like the others; rather, we keep alert and sober. . . . Therefore, encourage one another, and build one another up, each one

---

9. In other words, eschatology may be about ethics and morality as much as, maybe even *more than*, about the future. See the previous chapter.

the next one, just as you are already doing" (1 Thess 5:5-6; 11). What do we do in the face of an uncertain future? The next right thing. Rather than return evil for evil, we "always pursue the good (*agathon*), both for one another *and for everyone*" (5:15). This is the example of Jesus, and it marks those who imitate his way.

This is both a comfort and a warning.

DISCUSSION QUESTIONS

1. Are you by nature optimistic toward the future, or pessimistic? How does this stance affect how you think about God, the church, society, and the interactions between them?

2. Were ideas about the future (including the Second Coming and/or the "end of the world") prominent in your own up-bringing, whether in your family or your church or your broader social environment? Did those ideas produce a sense of fear of the future? Or did they nurture a feeling of confidence for the future?

3. Do present realities (cultural, religious, political, etc.) make you fearful or confident about the future? What do you worry about? What are you hopeful for?

4. How do ideas about eschatology (eternity, judgment and reward, heaven and hell, etc.) affect life here on earth, now in the present? How, in other words, is heaven *here*? How is eternity *now*?

5. What makes "doing the next right thing" hard? Or what makes recognizing "the next right thing" hard? On the other hand, what spurs you on to "doing the next right thing"?

6

"A LETTER CLAIMING TO BE FROM US"

Paul's Second Letter to the Thessalonians?

Whether or not Simon and Cleobius were welcome visitors depended on who you asked. By the look of things, many locals were enthusiastic about the arrival of these teachers, who seemed to have a knack for expressing the cherished beliefs of older saints in ways that also ignited the imaginations of younger believers. At the very least, no one could deny that Simon and Cleobius were generating a lot of interest.

On the other hand, not everyone was pleased with these newcomers. For some, the visitors' words sounded less like a fresh expression of the old faith and more like twists on the truth, or—to say the same thing with a different word—*un*truths. The new teachers were claiming that Israel's prophetic traditions were not actually the word of God. The resurrection to new life, they said, would not involve the flesh-and-blood bodies of believers. They even denied that Jesus actually experienced the birthing process, feeling the contractions of Mary's uterus and being pushed through the birth canal and out into the world. In fact, "the Lord"—it wasn't always clear if they were talking about Jesus or someone who just *seemed* like Jesus—wasn't actually a flesh-and-blood person.

Unsurprisingly, Simon and Cleobius's teaching was stirring up the gatherings of Jesus' followers in the city, and in response local elders decided to write to Paul, who was only about 450 miles away. Hopefully, Paul would be able to come and deal with these new teachers, refuting them where they were distorting the apostolic faith and correcting those who were attracted to their teachings. But even if he couldn't come in person, Paul was known to be a powerful and effective letter-writer, and maybe he could offer his wisdom—which seemed not to be his own—through pen and parchment.

The apostle did not disappoint. Though his letter is not long, we can't reproduce the whole thing here. But it gets right to the point and provides guidance on what to think about these new teachers (and, more importantly, what to *do* about them):

> Paul, the prisoner of Jesus Christ, to the brothers and sisters at Corinth—greeting!
>
> Being in many afflictions, I marvel not that the teachings of the evil one had such rapid success. For my Lord Jesus Christ will quickly come, since he is rejected by those who falsify his teaching. For I delivered to you first of all what I received from the apostles before me who were always with Jesus Christ, that our Lord Jesus Christ was born of Mary of the seed of David, the Father having sent the Spirit from heaven into her that he might come into this

world and save all flesh by his own flesh and that he might raise us in the flesh from the dead as he has presented himself to us as our example. And since human beings are created by their Father, for this reason they were sought by him when they were lost, to become alive by adoption....

And whoever accepts this rule which we have received by the blessed prophets and the holy gospel, shall receive a reward, but for whomsoever deviates from this rule fire shall be for him and for those who preceded him therein since they are Godless people, a generation of vipers. Resist them in the power of the Lord. Peace be with you.

* * *

There's just one problem: Paul never wrote this letter. This is the non-biblical letter known as *3 Corinthians*, written in the second century CE, about a hundred years after Paul was martyred by the Emperor Nero.[1] To be sure, *3 Corinthians* echoes elements of Paul's genuine letters. The letter's opening, when Paul refers to himself as "the prisoner of Jesus Christ," certainly evokes the memory of the opening of Paul's letter to Philemon: "Paul, a prisoner of Christ Jesus" (Phlm 1). The language of Paul, in which he declares that he "delivered to you first of all what I received," echoes his earlier words to the Corinthians: "For I passed on to you as of first importance that which I also received" (1 Cor 15:3; see also 11:23). The reference to the other apostles as being "apostles before me" might remind us of 1 Cor 15:7–9, where Paul describes the risen Jesus' appearances "to all the apostles" before mentioning the appearance "last of all" to Paul, "the least of the apostles." We could mention

---

1. Translations of *3 Corinthians* come from Elliott, *Apocryphal New Testament*, 380–82, with slight modifications.

others; for "our Lord Jesus Christ was born . . . of the seed of David," see Rom 1:3. For "born of Mary," see Gal 4:4 (which, we should note, does not mention Mary by name). For "adoption," see Rom 8:15; Gal 4:5 (also, Rom 9:4).

But there are also important differences between Paul's genuine letters and *3 Corinthians*, some subtle and some more obvious. These differences might be simple differences of expression or more complicated differences in theology. For example, *3 Corinthians* opens, "Paul, the prisoner of Jesus Christ, to the brethren at Corinth—greeting!" That last word in Greek is *chairein*, the standard way of opening ancient Greek letters (not unlike the way letters today typically begin, "Dear So-and-So").[2] None of Paul's letters, however, begins this way; Paul begins all his letters with some version of "Grace and peace to you" (e.g., 1 Thess 1:1), which in Greek sounds a little similar (compare *chairein* with *charis hymin kai eirene*). At the same time, some see a very different theology at work in *3 Corinthians*, which insists God will "raise us in the flesh from the dead," compared to Paul's own words, that "flesh and blood are not able to inherit the kingdom of God" (1 Cor 15:50).

These and other reasons persuade scholars that *3 Corinthians* is a *pseudepigraph*, or a "falsely inscribed" letter (*pseudēs*, "false," and *epigraphē*, "inscription"), written in the name of Paul but not *actually* by Paul. Pseudepigraphy was common among the early Christians, and not only among the early Christians. The early Christians wrote gospels and gospel-like texts under the names of famous apostles, such as Thomas, Peter, or James. They also wrote letters under the names of important figures like Paul,

---

2. Three letters in the New Testament begin with *chairein*. See the Jerusalem Council's letter in Acts 15:23–29, the military tribune's letter to Felix in Acts 23:26–30, and the New Testament letter of James (see Jas 1:1).

Barnabas, and even Christ himself. Did the authors intend to deceive their readers, as if they really were reading a gospel written by Thomas or a letter from Paul? Or did both authors and readers understand these false ascriptions as literary fictions, like the meme of Abraham Lincoln with the words, "Don't believe everything you read on the Internet just because there's a picture with a quote next to it"?[3] Scholars continue to debate these questions.

IS 2 THESSALONIANS "FALSELY INSCRIBED"?

Scholars largely—but not unanimously—agree that 1 Thessalonians was written before 2 Thessalonians. In the seventeenth century, Dutch Humanist Hugo Grotius (1583–1645) argued that 2 Thessalonians was written before 1 Thessalonians, a view one can find even today.[4] At the turn of the nineteenth century, German biblical scholarship in particular began to question the authenticity of 2 Thessalonians "virtually for the first time."[5] The issue was debated throughout the nineteenth century until, at the turn of the twentieth century, William Wrede (1859–1906) forcefully argued that 2 Thessalonians was written after Paul's death, in imitation of the style of 1 Thessalonians but largely "to correct or to oppose much in the First Letter."[6] Today, 2 Thessalonians is included among the so-called "disputed Pauline letters," which also include Ephesians, Colossians, and the three Pastoral Epistles (1–2 Timothy and Titus).

---

3. See Rodríguez, *Jesus Darkly*, 113–14.

4. For Grotius, see Thiselton, *Thessalonians*, 11–12. For a contemporary argument for the priority of 2 Thessalonians, see Wanamaker, *Thessalonians*, 37–45.

5. Thiselton, *Thessalonians*, 12–15 (p. 12 quoted).

6. Thiselton, *Thessalonians*, 13–14.

"A Letter Claiming to be from Us"

Disputed, of course, is different from *pseudepigraphal*. No one thinks Paul actually wrote *3 Corinthians*, so we can call this letter pseudepigraphal (remember: "falsely ascribed") and even refer to its author as "pseudo-Paul." But what about the letters in the New Testament that claim to be written by Paul, but that scholars are not so sure about? Should we refer to the author(s) of the Pastoral Epistles, or Ephesians, or 2 Thessalonians as "pseudo-Paul"?

Few people go this far. Among Pauline scholars, the disputed letters are often referred to as "deutero-Pauline," with *deutero* meaning something like "secondary" or "secondarily": these are "secondarily Pauline" letters. Paul-like. Paul-*ish*. The sense is that these letters represent Paul in some way, whether by applying his theology or reputation to a later situation after his death or co-opting his legacy for a later controversy. Some scholars see in deutero-Pauline letters an attempt to deceive the reader into accepting as coming from Paul something that Paul never wrote. Others see something less nefarious, perhaps some of Paul's companions or disciples writing in Paul's name and conveying the kinds of things Paul said when he was alive. And then, of course, some scholars see the disputed letters as actually written by Paul: these letters may be disputed, but the dispute is inconclusive or even wrong-headed. For scholars in this last group, Paul wrote all thirteen letters attributed to him in the New Testament. (This last is a minority position; few—not none, but few—Pauline scholars attribute all or even any of the Pastoral Epistles to Paul himself.) Many scholars fall somewhere in the middle: Paul may not have written all thirteen New Testament letters that bear his name, but he may have written some of the disputed letters.

This chapter is not a survey of the disputed letters attributed to Paul in the New Testament. This chapter is focused only on the question of 2 Thessalonians. Why do some scholars accept that Paul wrote 1 Thessalonians but doubt he wrote 2 Thessalonians? Why do other scholars accept Paul as the author of both letters? The most important question must certainly be: *Did* Paul write 2 Thessalonians? The present chapter will not be able to answer that last question. The scholars who dispute this letter do so based on real difficulties with the letter. They are not simply trying to question the Bible or undermine the Christian faith or anything like that. On the other hand, those challenges or difficulties are not so significant that they prove Paul *could not have written* 2 Thessalonians.

For my own part, I have not been convinced that Paul did not write 2 Thessalonians, but neither can I prove that he did. My goal for this chapter, then, is simply to lay out some of the arguments that have been offered over the last two-plus centuries regarding the authorship of 2 Thessalonians. Readers can decide for themselves which position seems most compelling, though I acknowledge up front that readers will be able to detect my own judgment that arguments against 2 Thessalonians' authenticity are not compelling.

THE THESSALONIAN LETTERS SIDE-BY-SIDE

Second Thessalonians was either written hot on the heels of 1 Thessalonians, perhaps just weeks or months after the first letter, or it was written decades later, after Paul was executed by Nero. Before we can decide which scenario is more likely, let's take stock of the letter and how it compares to its longer namesake.

The two letters begin almost identically, as you can see in table 6.1; words that are identical in 1 and 2 Thessalonians have been underlined:

1 Thess 1:1:	2 Thess 1:1-2:
<u>Paul and Silvanus and Timothy</u>. <u>To the assembly of the Thessalonians in God</u> the <u>Father and the Lord Jesus Christ</u>. <u>Grace and peace to you</u>.	<u>Paul and Silvanus and Timothy</u>. <u>To the assembly of the Thessalonians in God</u> our <u>Father and the Lord Jesus Christ</u>. <u>Grace and peace to you</u> from God our Father and the Lord Jesus Christ.

Table 6.1: The opening addresses of 1 and 2 Thessalonians

In addition to their nearly identical openings, both letters have longer-than-normal statements of thanksgiving (compare 1 Thess 1:2–10 and 2 Thess 1:3–12), called *thanksgiving periods*. Even more unusual, both letters seem to resume their thanksgiving later in the letter (compare 1 Thess 2:13 and 2 Thess 2:13–14). This is not common.

The Thessalonian letters also share a number of themes. Perhaps most conspicuously, both letters are especially concerned with questions about eschatology and Jesus' *parousia* ("presence, arrival, coming"; see 1 Thess 4:13—5:11 and 2 Thess 2:1–12).[7] Jesus' *parousia* dominates large sections of both letters and is associated with other, similar ideas (like the "day of the Lord"; see 1 Thess 5:2; 2 Thess 2:2). Despite this similarity, scholars have noticed an important difference in the two letters regarding the expectations for Jesus' arrival:[8]

---

7. See the previous chapter.

8. In English, 1 Thess 5:3 and 2 Thess 2:3 both have the word *destruction*. This word is not underlined in the table, however, because the Greek texts use two different words: *olethros* in 1 Thess 5:3, and *apōleia* in 2 Thess 2:3.

1 Thess 5:1–3:	2 Thess 2:3–5:
But you do not need to have anything written to you, brothers and sisters, concerning ages and seasons, for you yourselves are well aware that the day of the Lord is coming like a thief at night. Even as they say, "Peace and safety," then destruction suddenly comes upon them, the way labor comes to a pregnant woman, and they will have no means of escape.	Let no one deceive you in any way; the day of the Lord will not come until the rebellion comes and the man of lawlessness is revealed—that is, the son of destruction, who opposes and exalts himself over every so-called god or deity, for which reason he sits in the sanctuary of God, even proclaiming that he himself is a god. Do you not remember that I was saying these things to you when I was still with you?

Table 6.2: The arrival of "the day of the Lord" in 1 and 2 Thessalonians

In 1 Thessalonians, Jesus' arrival (*parousia*) and the day of the Lord arrive suddenly, unexpectedly, "like a thief at night" or the sudden—though hopefully not *completely* unexpected—onset of labor pains. Second Thessalonians seems to have a different scenario in mind, where a series of signs precedes and even heralds the imminent arrival of the day of the Lord: first, "the one who restrains" "the man of lawlessness" will need to be removed, which will result, second, in the revelation of that "man of lawlessness" (2 Thess 2:3, 6–8). The man of lawlessness's arrival (*parousia*!) will be accompanied by false miracles and signs and wonders, but in the end (on the day of the Lord?) he will be destroyed by "the breath of his [i.e., Jesus'] mouth," along with everyone who did not "accept the love of truth" but instead was deceived by the man of lawlessness (2:9–12).

A second broad theme shared by 1 and 2 Thessalonians concerns work, or labor, both the apostles' labor among the

Thessalonians and the Thessalonians' ongoing labor despite their hope in Jesus' imminent arrival. First Thessalonians opens with references to the "work of [the readers'] faith" and "the labor of [their] love" (1 Thess 1:3), which is not unlike the prayer in 2 Thessalonians for the readers to desire "goodness and faithful work in power" (2 Thess 1:11). In both letters the authors refer to their example among the Thessalonians:

1 Thess 2:9	2 Thess 3:8:
For you remember, brothers and sisters, our <u>labor and toil</u>: <u>night and day we were at work so that we would not be a burden on you in any way</u>; we proclaimed to you the gospel of God.	Instead, by <u>labor and toil</u>, <u>night and day we were at work so that we would not be a burden on you in any way</u>.

Table 6.3: "Labor and toil" in 1 and 2 Thessalonians

The phrase "labor and toil" is not common; it occurs in these two Thessalonian passages, with the positive connotation of self-sufficiency, and in 2 Cor 11:27, with a negative connotation of suffering. More importantly, both Thessalonian passages share an extended phrase with verbatim agreement over ten words in Greek: "night and day we were at work so that we would not be a burden on you in any way." Such a lengthy agreement suggests an intention to copy verbatim the wording of another text. Some scholars see here an example of a later writer or writers copying from Paul and Silvanus and Timothy's letter to the Thessalonians; others see an example of Paul and Silvanus and Timothy copying the phrasing from their first letter in their second. Even beyond this one phrase, however, both letters stress the importance of work and labor, both for self-sufficiency and for the community's reputation with others (1 Thess 3:9; 4:11–12; 2 Thess 3:7–13).

Besides major themes like the *parousia* of Jesus or the value and function of labor, these letters also share smaller, more localized themes. For example, both letters are concerned with "disorderly" behavior in the community.

1 Thess 5:14:	2 Thess 3:6–7, 11:
But we urge you, brothers and sisters: instruct the <u>disorderly</u>; console the weary; devote yourselves to the needs of the weak; be patient toward everyone.	But we command you, brothers and sisters, in the name of our Lord Jesus Christ, to keep yourselves from every <u>disorderly</u> brother or sister who has forsaken the tradition that they received from us. For you yourselves know how you ought to imitate us, and that we were not <u>disorderly</u> among you. . . . For we are hearing reports of some people among you who live <u>disorderly</u> lives, not keeping busy but rather being busy bodies.

Table 6.4: "Disorderly" in 1 and 2 Thessalonians

The word *disorderly*, in Greek, is *ataktos*, and it could refer to soldiers who were undisciplined, non-military persons who were immoral, or music that could not keep a beat. First Thessalonians may seem to be more patient toward these undisciplined or immoral (or un-musical!) people; Paul and Silvanus and Timothy tell their readers to admonish or instruct them. At first blush 2 Thessalonians seems to take a harder line: now the readers are told to keep away from them and instead to follow the example Paul and his companions set when they were in Thessalonica. I say "at first blush" because the second letter also offers instructions for the disorderly. Immediately after the passage cited in table 6.4, the authors continue: "To people like this [i.e., the disorderly], we command and encourage in the Lord Jesus Christ, that by working peaceably they might earn their own bread. As for you, brothers and sisters, do not grow weary in doing good" (2 Thess 3:12–13). This stance is not so different from what we find in 1 Thessalonians.

Another theme shared by these two letters concerns imitation, or following the example of the apostles:

1 Thess 1:6–7; 2:14:	2 Thess 3:7–9:
So you became <u>imitators</u> of us and of the Lord, by receiving the word amid considerable affliction, along with the joy of the holy Spirit so that you became an example for everyone who believes, throughout Macedonia as well as Achaia. . . . For you became <u>imitators</u>, brothers and sisters, of the assemblies of God that are in Christ Jesus in the region of Judea, for you suffered the same kinds of things even at the hands of your own people, just as they suffered even at the hands of their fellow Jews.	For you yourselves know how you ought to <u>imitate</u> us, and that we were not disorderly among you, nor did we take bread from anyone without paying for it. Instead, by toil and labor, night and day, we worked so that we would not be a burden on you in any way. Not that we did not have the right, but we labored so that we could present ourselves to you as an example, for you to <u>imitate</u> us.

Table 6.5: "Imitate" in 1 and 2 Thessalonians

Imitation, or what scholars call *mimesis*, is not a common theme in the Pauline epistles. The word *imitator* only occurs three other times in the letters attributed to Paul, twice in the much longer 1 Corinthians (see 1 Cor 4:16; 11:1) and once in Ephesians, a disputed Pauline letter (see Eph 5:1). To have two references to imitation in each of these comparatively short letters is striking. The terms and how the authors use them are not quite identical in these letters. There are two noticeable differences. In 1 Thessalonians, the authors use the noun *imitator* (Greek: *mimētēs*), while 2 Thessalonians uses the verb, *imitate* (Greek: *mimeomai*). Also, 1 Thessalonians mentions three examples for imitation: "us" and "the Lord" in 1:6, and Jewish believers in Judea in 2:14. In 2 Thessalonians, the only example to be imitated is "us" (i.e., Paul, Silvanus, and Timothy).

We could mention a number of other similarities between 1 and 2 Thessalonians, including the concern for being "worthy" of "the kingdom of God" (1 Thess 2:12; 2 Thess 1:5), or the repeated mentions of "afflictions" or "suffering" (1 Thess 1:6; 2:14; 3:3–7; 2 Thess 1:4–7), or the call to "remember" the apostles' example or words (1 Thess 2:9; 2 Thess 2:5), or frequent references to "instructions" and/or "encouragement," and so on. Hopefully, however, we have said enough to show that 1 and 2 Thessalonians have a lot in common, but that even some of those commonalities show some interesting or potentially significant differences (especially regarding Jesus' *parousia*, and the different uses of the language of "imitation").

EVALUATING THE THESSALONIAN LETTERS' SIMILARITIES AND DIFFERENCES

So how should we evaluate these similarities and differences? The eschatological section of 2 Thessalonians begins with a note of encouragement that, no, Jesus' *parousia* and "the day of the Lord" have not already taken place, and the Thessalonians have not missed out on the object of their hope.

> So we ask you, brothers and sisters, with regards to the *parousia* of our Lord Jesus Christ and of

> our gathering together with him, that you not be easily shaken, nor your mind be troubled, neither by a spirit nor a word nor a letter claiming to be from us that alleges that the day of the Lord has already come. (2 Thess 2:1–2)

That line in v. 2—"neither by a spirit nor a word *nor a letter claiming to be from us*"—has caught scholars' attention, along with the unusual claim at the end of the letter: "This is the greeting I write in my own hand: From Paul. This is my sign in every letter, just as I've written here" (3:17). For many readers, these features of 2 Thessalonians are ironic, meant to verify the authenticity of an inauthentic letter.[9] Such features presume that letters written in Paul's name but not by Paul's hand are being distributed when 2 Thessalonians was written. Eugene Boring doubts that letters falsely attributed to Paul were circulating during his lifetime, so the reference in 2 Thess 2:2 to such letters is evidence that 2 Thessalonians likely comes from a generation or two after Paul's death.[10] I am not so confident. In a world where books were copied by hand and where teachers' lectures could be published from notes taken by students, the possibility of a quasi- or pseudo-Pauline letter circulating even during Paul's own lifetime is not at all difficult to imagine.[11] (Paul may not have provided a handwritten greeting in all of his letters, but see Gal 6:11: "Look at what large letters I wrote to you with my own hand!")

---

9. "Some scholars suggest that the writer of 2 Thessalonians 'doth protest too much' and that this is a signal that the letter is forged. Although it is meant to reassure the readers that the letter is genuine (in contrast to the letter mentioned in 2.2), it is equally forged" (Ascough, *Thessalonians*, 59).

10. Boring, *Thessalonians*, 220–21.

11. Alexander, *Preface to Luke's Gospel*, 194n8; Alexander, "Ancient Book Production," 71–112. See also Brookins, *Thessalonians*, 141, 202–3.

The arguments that 2 Thessalonians was written by one of Paul's students, or perhaps someone who belonged to a "Pauline school" after the apostle's death, are not baseless. At the end of the day, there are two peculiar facts that require explanation. First, 2 Thessalonians bears striking resemblance to 1 Thessalonians, including following the same basic structure (which differs from the structure of the other undisputed Pauline letters), taking up at least some of the same themes of the first letter (Jesus' *parousia*, enduring suffering, and how to deal with the "disorderly"), and using much of the same vocabulary.[12] Second, 2 Thessalonians nevertheless has a number of distinctive ideas and uses some of its important language differently. Scholars who see 2 Thessalonians as written by someone other than Paul—usually a student of Paul, or a student of a student of Paul, rather than some random author with no connection to the Pauline tradition—point to these differences to support their claim that 2 Thessalonians was written by someone other than Paul. They explain the similarities, then, as the author imitating Paul, probably using 1 Thessalonians as a model or a framework for his own pseudepigraphal letter. On the other hand, scholars who see 2 Thessalonians as written by Paul (and Silvanus and Timothy) point to the similarities to support their claim that 2 Thessalonians was written by the same author(s) as 1 Thessalonians. They explain the differences, then, as the result of writing a (slightly) different letter in the aftermath of the first letter.

What should we make of these observations? Some scholars, reading from good faith, see the letter as a product of some of Paul's followers (or some of his followers'

---

12. For the return to themes from 1 Thessalonians, see Boring, *Thessalonians*, 211. Of the 249 different Greek words in the NA[28], Greek New Testament text of 2 Thessalonians, over 160 of those words (nearly 65%) also occur in 1 Thessalonians.

followers), writing to update the legacy of Paul for a later generation and a new situation.[13] Others, also reading from good faith, see the letter as a follow-up to the first letter, either to clarify the contents of the first or to respond to reports of the Thessalonians' response to that first letter.[14] The answer to the question of authenticity isn't as arbitrary as tossing a coin, but the surviving evidence is susceptible to either conclusion. Timothy Brookins speculates that, if scholars were polled on the question of 2 Thessalonians' authorship, that poll "would likely indicate that those neither for nor against could claim a true majority."[15] In other words, Brookins thinks the majority of scholars would confess they do not know who wrote 2 Thessalonians. I think he is probably right.

Since the evidence for or against Pauline authorship is inconclusive, we should hold our view of 2 Thessalonians' authenticity with a healthy dose of humility. Two considerations move me to lean toward the view that Paul did, in fact, write this letter, whether directly or in collaboration with co-authors (viz., Silvanus and Timothy), or indirectly through a delegate. First, as mentioned above, doubt about 2 Thessalonians' authorship did not arise until around 1800; until then, the church was unanimous in its judgment that 2 Thessalonians was a genuine letter of Paul's. To be sure, the church is capable of being wrong about these kinds of things; until the Renaissance, many Christians accepted as genuine a "falsely inscribed" (pseudepigraphal) series of letters between Paul and the Roman philosopher Seneca

---

13. For an insightful, sensitive, and nuanced expression of this perspective, see Boring, *Thessalonians*.

14. For an insightful, sensitive, and nuanced expression of this perspective, see Brookins, *Thessalonians*.

15. Brookins, *Thessalonians*, 138–47 (p. 139 quoted).

the Younger.¹⁶ But the church did express skepticism about certain texts, including some texts that would eventually be included in the New Testament canon (e.g., 2 Peter, Jude, and others) and many that would not (including *3 Corinthians*). By the time the early Christians were discussing which texts were *canonical* (from Greek *kanōn*, "reed, measure," and so, metaphorically, "rule, standard"), they seem already to have concluded that a collection of Paul's letters ought to be included within the canon, and they seem unanimously to have included 2 Thessalonians within that collection.¹⁷ The fact that no one in the ancient church questioned the authorship of 2 Thessalonians, as far as we know, is a pebble tipping the scale ever so slightly in favor of authenticity.¹⁸

More significant, however, is the problem of identifying a reason for someone to write 2 Thessalonians in Paul's name sometime after Paul's death. We noted in chapter 1 that letters are "occasional texts"; they speak to a unique circumstance and address particular problems or pursue specific goals. No matter what we think about 2 Thessalonians' authorship and date, we have to explain why an author should write *this* particular letter to *this* particular audience addressing *this* particular set of questions. The most common explanation offered for 2 Thessalonians is the concern for "the delay of Jesus' *parousia*." That is, the first generation of Christians expected Jesus' *parousia* at any moment, an expectation expressed in the phrase "we who remain alive until the *parousia* of the Lord" in 1 Thess

---

16. See Gray, "Apocryphal Pauline Literature," in *DPL*² 43.

17. "The origins of the collected Pauline letters are obscure," notes Harry Gamble, though he also observes "broad agreement that a more or less full collection had come into existence by the late years of the first century" (Gamble, *Books and Readers*, 59). See also Gallagher and Meade, *Biblical Canon Lists*, 39–44.

18. See Gupta, *Thessalonians*, 214–15.

4:15. But once that generation began to die out—including Paul, who likely was martyred sometime between 62 and 68 CE—Christians had to rework their earlier expectations for the future to accommodate the longer-than-expected arrival of the end. The problem with this explanation, however, is that 2 Thessalonians is not a general letter about an uncertain future. It addresses the concerns of a specific community, including concerns about present suffering and members who apparently refuse to work. New Testament scholar Nijay Gupta notes, "Until those who label 2 Thessalonians a forgery are able to construct a convincing scenario that would necessitate such a pseudepigraphal letter, it seems more responsible to treat this text as a genuine Pauline letter, warts and all."[19] "More responsible" might be a bit strong; there are indeed literary warts on the face of 2 Thessalonians, and theories of pseudonymity are not *irresponsible*. Even so, I agree with Gupta's judgment about this letter: it is sufficiently "Pauline" to justify reading it as an expression of Paul's thoughts, and the questions about its authorship are not sufficiently compelling to move me to read it, like 3 *Corinthians*, as pseudo-Paul.

SECOND THESSALONIANS AS SCRIPTURE

In a letter Paul will write a few years after 1 (and 2) Thessalonians, Paul says, "In my [former] letter, I wrote to you not to have anything to do with sexually immoral persons" (1 Cor 5:9). That (former) letter no longer exists. The possibility of "lost scriptures" coming to light and altering or even upending cherished Christian beliefs regularly excites or inflames public imagination. In 2012, a forged papyrus fragment was published with the words, "Jesus said to them, 'my wife. . . .'" Though no respectable historian or

19. Gupta, *Thessalonians*, 220.

theologian thought this text would prove the historical Jesus had been married, the idea that at least one group of early Christians portrayed him as having a wife would have had remarkable consequences for our view of the diversity of earliest Christianity. That papyrus fragment, called "The Gospel of Jesus's Wife," created quite a sensation in the media and in popular culture. In the end, the fragment turned out to be hoax, and the scholar most closely associated with endorsing its authenticity took a hit to her reputation.[20]

And yet . . . we know the early Christians wrote texts we have never seen. Including a letter from Paul to the Corinthians, written *before* 1 Corinthians. How could we *not* be intrigued?

Second Thessalonians is a different problem: not a lost, previously unknown text but a letter we have always known, now with some questions as to its origin. What if it turns out that Paul *didn't* write 2 Thessalonians? Was the church wrong to include it in the New Testament canon? Should we remove it from our copies of the Bible?

I don't know of anyone who seriously argues we should remove any of the disputed Pauline letters from the New Testament. Questions about authorship are *historical* questions, while questions of canonicity are *theological* questions. The two are not unrelated, of course, but neither are they identical. Even if 2 Thessalonians *were* written by one or more of Paul's associates or disciples, the church believed that Luke-Acts was written by Paul's associate, Luke (hence the name: "The Gospel According to Luke"). So no, I don't think the church was wrong to include 2 Thessalonians in the New Testament, even if I agreed that 2 Thessalonians was written by someone else, some years after Paul's death.

---

20. For the fascinating (and tragic) story of "The Gospel of Jesus's Wife," see Sabar, *Veritas*.

"A Letter Claiming to be from Us"

But the church is wrong in a different way. We might not excise 2 Thessalonians from the Bible, but we excise it from our study of the Bible, from our preaching, and from our understanding of being the people of God in the world. This is not an accusation; it is a confession. My own interest in the Thessalonian correspondence was aroused a few years ago when I had to teach these letters to first-year undergraduate students and I realized that, despite having something of a reputation as a Pauline scholar, I knew next to nothing about either letter addressed to the Thessalonians. In some ways, this book is an act of penance. My motivation is not so much to atone for any purported sin—not reading the Thessalonian letters is rather low on my list of moral, interpersonal, and spiritual failings—as it is to receive what God or the church might have to offer anyone who allows themselves to experience them.

Second Thessalonians will never be as heady as Romans or as practical as 1 Corinthians, and so it will never be as interesting as those longer letters. And yet, in a world that so eagerly detaches itself from the obligations and inheritance of past generations, perhaps 2 Thessalonians offers us an important reminder that what we have received from the past can provide a surer footing for facing an uncertain present or future. "So then, brothers and sisters, stand firm and hold on to the traditions that you were taught, whether by speech or by a letter from us. May our Lord Jesus Christ himself, and God our Father, who graciously loved us and gave us eternal comfort and good hope, encourage your hearts and strengthen you by every good work and word" (2 Thess 2:15–17). Sure, our forebears fell well short of being perfect, and we will sometimes make different moral, cultural, even religious choices than they did. Even so, we would do well to live up to their desires for us: "the Lord is faithful; he will strengthen you and keep you from evil. So we are persuaded by the Lord for you, that you are already doing and will do those things that we are commanding you. May the Lord direct your hearts to the love of God and to the endurance of Christ" (2 Thess 3:3–5).

Amen.

DISCUSSION QUESTIONS

1. What do you think of the early Christians' practice of writing texts (gospels, letters, etc.) and attributing them to significant and/or popular figures? Is this practice deceptive, or is it a way of applying a person's legacy or reputation to new questions?
2. How do questions of authorship and pseudonymity intersect with questions of authority and canonicity? Can letters that claim to be written by Paul be included in the Bible if they weren't actually written by Paul?
3. What similarities do you see between 1 and 2 Thessalonians? In what ways does 2 Thessalonians guide or confirm your interpretation of 1 Thessalonians?
4. What differences do you see between 1 and 2 Thessalonians? In what ways does 2 Thessalonians change or challenge your interpretation of 1 Thessalonians?
5. What inspiration or wisdom—if any—do you see in these shorter books of the New Testament that don't get as much attention as their longer counterparts?

7

HOSPITALITY
Welcoming Another as an Other

As A POLITICAL OR cultural issue, *xenophobia*—a fear and/or hatred of persons or things strange or foreign, from the Greek words *xenos* ("stranger, foreigner") and *phobos* ("fear, terror")—is a problem on the Right. In both American and European political discourse, any ideology that seeks to heighten the distinctions between nations and their populaces and brighten the lines between them is defined as right-wing. On both sides of the Atlantic Ocean, individuals and groups on the Right seek to protect national integrity and stability by restricting the influx of temporary or permanent immigrants, or both. Their political and ideological opponents on the Left advocate policies they portray as more welcoming to foreigners, immigrants, and refugees, including the creation of "sanctuary jurisdictions": cities, counties, or whole states that refuse to cooperate with immigration enforcement agencies and their personnel.

Almost by definition, then, xenophobia is a problem on the Right.

Except that xenophobia is in no way a problem only on the Right. Individuals and groups on the Left—whether in the United States or in Europe, and probably everywhere on earth—find themselves no less capable than their counterparts on the Right of ostracizing outsiders, silencing dissent, and enforcing norms of both speech and behavior. Bill Bishop opened his 2008 book, *The Big Sort*, by describing his and his wife's serendipitous move to a neighborhood in Austin, Texas. "We didn't intend to move into a community filled with Democrats, but that's what we did—effortlessly and without a trace of understanding about what we were doing." The neighborhood was a good fit for them, and they for it. He describes it as "one of the friendliest I've encountered." And in such a homogenous community, even the most contentious and cantankerous topics became avenues—even *autobahns*—for strengthening communal ties. "Far from avoiding politics as a topic of discussion in neighborly talks, Travis Heights encourages it. . . . Our like-mindedness was a comfort, a shortcut to intimacy."

Unless you were Stephen Mason, the "one Republican" and "lone conservative" on the neighborhood listserv. When Stephen expressed his support for a local, "deeply conservative" candidate, his political expression had to be dealt with. "Mason wasn't just someone to be argued against. For the protection of the group, he needed to be isolated, sealed off, and expelled." Not everyone who disagreed with Stephen wanted him silenced, of course. But, as often happens in online forums, those that did won out. Stephen "was a Republican Crusoe on this Democratic island, and so he withdrew, promising never to talk politics again with his neighbors."[1]

1. Bishop, *Big Sort*, 1–5.

Hospitality

It would be as wrong to suggest xenophobia is a problem endemic to Democratic spaces and not to Republican ones as it would be to suggest Republicans but not Democrats can be unwelcoming people. That's actually the point. Social homogeneity greases the touchpoints of social interaction, making encounters with neighbors and strangers alike more predictable and less subject to conflict. When we all share key social values and norms, our social space feels "ours." Threats to the "our-ness" of that space provoke a response, the social analog of the antibody response to the presence of foreign agents in the human body. If I may speak in an extreme generality for one moment, conservatives in small towns or rural spaces and progressives in urban or elite spaces both enjoy being in the majority in their social spheres, and both are capable of taking action to protect their status. Both, in other words, are capable of expressing xenophobic thoughts and/or exhibiting xenophobic behaviors toward strangers, outsiders, people who don't belong. Both are also capable of remarkable acts of hospitality. And not just in the aggregate: *individuals*— conservative, progressive, and all else besides—are capable of immense generosity and shocking inhumanity. We, for good *and* for ill, contain multitudes.

Contemporary Western cultures generally espouse diversity, pluralism, and multiculturalism as values to be lauded, even if the actual living out of those values is more elusive and difficult than we would like to admit. It is rare to encounter actual arguments against diversity, even if resistance to and reactions against diversity are unfortunately common. It is almost as if we all agree diversity is good and uniformity is bad, but then for reasons we are not quite able to articulate we find it difficult to embody a generosity toward strangers—that is, not people unknown to us but rather people who are *strange* to us. Diversity, though often sought-out and celebrated, is like grit in the social machinery, creating friction in and raising the temperature of interactions between people who have different worldviews. Sometimes that grit causes the gears to seize. This is not an argument against diversity or openness to others; it is rather a recognition that diversity and pluralism have a social cost.

In this chapter, we will consider the Christian value of *hospitality*, or the reception of, welcome, and care for strangers. If *xenophobia* refers to a fear and/or hatred of persons or things strange or foreign, hospitality is its opposite, its antonym. *Hospitality* translates the Greek word *philoxenia*, from *philos* ("friend, dear one") and *xenos* ("stranger, foreigner"). The Pastoral Epistles list hospitality as an expectation of the community's leaders (1 Tim 3:2; Titus 1:8), and the Petrine author urges his readers to "be hospitable toward one another without grumbling" (1 Pet 4:9). Paul tells the Romans to "pursue hospitality" (Rom 12:13). Perhaps most famously, the author to the Hebrews tells his readers, "Your love for one another must continue. Do not falter in showing hospitality, for by so doing some did not realize they were hosting angels" (Heb 13:1–2). Although neither 1 nor 2 Thessalonians uses the word *philoxenia*, the idea, as we will see, provides one of the Thessalonian letters' most important contributions to Christian thought and practice.

DEFINING *HOSPITALITY*

The New Testament authors use the word *philoxenia* in different ways. First Peter, in charging readers to "be hospitable toward one another without grumbling" (1 Pet 4:9), directs hospitality inward, toward other members of the community. The focus here is on welcoming other Christians, perhaps other local believers or possibly Christians who were traveling from out of town. If the point is to welcome local believers, we might further infer that some local believers are in precarious situations, perhaps even literally homeless.[2] Alternatively, given the likelihood that Christians were gathering in each others' homes or in the home of a host or hostess (see Rom 16:5), the point may be to encourage unity among local believers rather than choosing to meet with some Christians and refusing to meet with others. The author to the Hebrews seems also to think of hospitality as a virtue directed inward toward the church, toward other believers.

This is not exactly how Paul thinks about hospitality. For Paul, hospitality is a virtue directed both inward and outward, both toward other Christians and also beyond the boundaries of the community. The Pastoral Epistles are unclear, both because the texts do not explain whom prospective elders should welcome and because the Pastoral Epistles are the most disputed of the canonical letters attributed to Paul.[3] In the only occurrence of *philoxenia* in the undisputed Pauline letters, Romans 12 urges readers to persist in doing good even in the midst of opposition and suffering, assisting fellow believers in their afflictions and resisting the temptation to return hostility for hostility:

> Love must be sincere. Hate what is evil; cling to what is good. Be devoted to one another in brotherly love, and hold each other in greater honor. Do not shrink back from showing diligence. Be enthusiastic in spirit. Serve the Lord. Rejoice in hope, endure suffering, and persevere in prayer. Shoulder the needs of the saints, and pursue hospitality. Bless those who persecute you; bless, and do not curse them. Be joyful with

2. This was the thesis of an important work on 1 Peter; see Elliott, *Home for the Homeless*.

3. See the previous chapter.

the joyful; mourn with the mournful. (Rom 12:9–15)

Two things stick out from this paragraph and its larger context. First, like 1 Peter and Hebrews, Paul addresses how Christians—the "one body in Christ" (Rom 12:5)—ought to treat one another. The two key words, which we saw in an earlier chapter, are *love* (*agapē*) and *the good* (*agathon*): Christians are to live lives characterized by these rather ambiguous values (*love* and *the good*); doing so satisfies, for them, the requirements of Israel's Torah (see Rom 13:8–10).[4] In this paragraph, each of these instructions fleshes out what *love* and *the good* look like: devotion in brotherly love, the mutual demonstration of honor, and so on. Perhaps the most striking instructions are found in vv. 13 and 15: "shoulder the needs of the saints; . . . be joyful with the joyful; mourn with the mournful." In Romans 12, Paul urges his Roman readers to direct hospitality inward, toward the community, and not to neglect one another.

The second thing that sticks out, however, is Paul's orientation toward outsiders. Paul presumes hostility and antagonism from outsiders, so he encourages his readers toward endurance and perseverance (Rom 12:12). Beyond just "putting up with" hostile or antagonistic neighbors, however, Paul pushes his readers to bless their abusive neighbors, even repeating, "bless, and do not curse them" (12:14). The next paragraph expands on this idea: "Do not repay anyone evil for evil. Give careful thought for what is good in the sight of all the people. If it is within your power, make peace with everyone" (12:17–18). These are instructions for dealing not with other Christians but with outsiders, people beyond the bounds of the community. The point is not that Christians should simply accept injustice

---

4. See chapter 4.

and mistreatment; instead, they should trust that God sees and will rectify injustice, which in turn frees them to repay love for hatred and good for evil.

In the midst of all this is Rom 12:13b: "pursue hospitality." *Philoxenia*, according to Paul, defines how Jesus' followers relate both to insiders and outsiders. Hospitality is not simply an intra-group virtue, a way of clarifying and enforcing the line between who's in and who's out. Hospitality is *transgressive*; it violates the line between in and out and treats outsiders *as if they were insiders*. This makes hospitality enormously difficult, even dangerous. On a biological level, bodies are structured to police the boundary between inside and outside, to monitor what enters the body, and to respond aggressively when contaminants manage to slip through its defenses. This policing involves physical structures, including the ability to constrict or restrict the body's openings, hairs around nasal and ocular openings, and especially the skin encasing the entire body. This policing also includes *psychological* aspects, in which potentially harmful elements from outside the body evoke disgust and, if they get into the body, elicit an expulsive response (e.g., spitting or vomiting).[5] The thought of consuming roadkill or saliva—even our own!—triggers a disgust response. So also do social and moral contagions, like Stephen Mason, the deviant Republican in Bill Bishop's Democratic neighborhood, or George Orwell's malodorous masses.[6] Welcoming outsiders as if they were insiders is dangerous, like blindly eating mushrooms or drinking stagnant water. Both are

5. Richard Beck (*Unclean*, especially chapters 1–2) explains the biological and—tragically—social dynamics of disgust and its expulsive tendencies. While Beck's work has been largely well-received among Christian readers, we must acknowledge, reject, and condemn its antisemitic and supersessionist tropes. See Thiessen, *Jesus and the Forces of Death*, 1–5 (Thiessen cites Beck, *Unclean*, on p. 4).

6. See chapter 4.

liable to introduce foreign, alien, even dangerous or toxic agents into the body, and we are biologically and sociologically conditioned to protect against this very thing.

And yet, this seems to be at the very heart of Paul's definition of *philoxenia*, of hospitality: opening up the body of Christ to the risk of contamination and contagion, trusting that the example of Christ is to bless one's persecutors (Rom 12:14; see Luke 6:28) and the righteousness of God is to leave room for repentance and to avenge injustice (see Rom 2:4–5; 12:19–20). To be sure, Paul is certainly capable of exhibiting an expulsive response to people inside the community who pose a moral threat to the church (see 1 Cor 5:2, 13). In Romans 12, however, even in the midst of acknowledging real danger from people outside, Paul instructs his readers not to use that danger as an excuse to withhold hospitality from strangers.

FINDING HOSPITALITY IN THE THESSALONIAN LETTERS

Can we find these ideas in the Thessalonian correspondence, Paul's earliest letters, written to gentile converts in Thessalonica, who have abandoned their traditional, pagan forms of piety and cultic worship that satisfied the gods and averted their wrath? While Paul and Silvanus and Timothy do not use the word *philoxenia* in these letters, they do exhibit the very same ideas we saw in Romans 12. We can begin with three unnecessary words in the authors' prayer at the end of 1 Thessalonians 3. "May the Lord cause you to grow and increase in love for one another *and for everyone*, just as we are experiencing for you, in order to set your hearts blameless in holiness before our God and Father in the *parousia* of our Lord Jesus, with all his holy ones. Amen" (1 Thess 3:12–13). Once again, as we saw in chapter

4, the defining matrix of Pauline ethics is love (*agapē*), and the authors' prayer is for their ex-pagan pagan readers to experience this love in ever-increasing measures.[7]

The three unnecessary words in this prayer are "and for everyone," or in Greek, *kai eis pantas*. Not that these words are unimportant; they might even be the most important words in this prayer. But if they weren't there, if Paul and his co-authors had simply wrote, "may the Lord cause you to grow and increase in love for one another," we would not have thought it in any way odd. Paul and his companions had been worried that the Thessalonians were succumbing to pressure from outsiders to abandon their faith in Israel's God and her Messiah and reverting to their previous forms of pagan piety, but then they learned from Timothy that, in fact, the Thessalonians are steadfast in their devotion to God and to Christ and in their love for Paul and his companions. We would not be surprised, then, if the authors prayed that God would add to and increase (*pleonazō* and *perisseuō*) the bonds of love that unite these Christians, both to each other and to the authors.

The words *and for everyone* take that reasonable, expected abundance of love for the Christian community and aim it outward, beyond the boundaries of the ingroup.[8] These are not necessarily friendly, charitable outsiders for whom hospitality should come easily. The Thessalonians are experiencing opposition for abandoning their native

---

7. The authors use two words associated with increase and abundance: *pleonazō* and *perisseuō*. According to Malherbe (*Letters to the Thessalonians*, 212), these words "are synonymous and are used together for the sake of emphasis (so also in 2 Cor 4:15; Rom 5:20)."

8. The concept of an *ingroup* (and its opposite, *outgroup*) come from "social identity theory," a post-World War II theory that explains intra- and inter-group behaviors. For a survey of the research and its application to the New Testament, see Tucker and Baker, eds., *T&T Clark Handbook to Social Identity*.

worship, which kept the gods happy and friendly. To their neighbors' dismay, the Thessalonian Christians now worship the foreign God of a foreign people. Their conversion came "amid considerable affliction" from their neighbors (1 Thess 1:6; see also 2:14), and the authors will later express confidence that God will reward the Thessalonians for their enduring faith despite their suffering (2 Thess 1:3–7). In other words, beyond the boundaries of the community, the Thessalonian Christians have real enemies to worry about. But rather than pray a "hedge of protection" around the Thessalonian church from its enemies, Paul and Silvanus and Timothy pray for the Thessalonians to grow and increase in *agapē* for one another *kai eis pantas*, "and for everyone."

Even though we developed our definition of "hospitality" from Romans 12, and even though Paul and his co-authors never use the word *philoxenia* in the letters to the Thessalonians, the same notion of hospitality is clearly present in the prayer at the end of 1 Thessalonians 3. This idea of hospitality is even clearer in the next chapter:

> But you do not need anyone to write you about your love for one another, for you yourselves have been instructed by God to love one another; even now you are doing this very thing for all your brothers and sisters throughout all of Macedonia. So we encourage you, brothers and sisters, to progress all the more, to strive to live peaceably, to attend to your own affairs, and to work with your own hands, as we instructed you, so that you would conduct yourselves with decency *toward those outside* and would lack for nothing. (1 Thess 4:9–12)

As I mentioned in chapter 4, the phrase "love for one another" translates the Greek word *philadelphia*, a word that evokes the kind of love siblings have for one another (hence Philadelphia, the "City of Brotherly Love"). If taken literally, it might be construed narrowly in terms of welcoming fellow Christians and/or urging unity in the church. And certainly *philadelphia* in 1 Thessalonians 4 refers to the internal, intra-community love that Paul and his companions are praising among their Macedonian readers. But just as in Romans 12, where the words *philadelphia* and *philoxenia* are used in the span of just a few verses (see Rom 12:10 and 13, respectively), so here the "sibling-love" of the Thessalonians for one another is also aimed beyond the church, "toward those outside." The language of "progressing all the more" in 4:10 is the same language of abundance that we saw in 3:12; both passages have in view the increase or abundance of love directed inward and of love directed outward.

The clearest evocation in 1 Thessalonians of Paul's idea of *philoxenia* in Romans 12, however, comes in chapter 5. As we have seen on more than one occasion, the love and welcome of the community is nurtured inward even as it is also aimed outward. Not just fellow Christians, and not just friendly outsiders, but even potentially and/or actually hostile outsiders are the objects of the Thessalonians' hospitality. So, for insiders: "acknowledge those who labor among you and rule over you in the Lord, and who instruct you; respect them beyond all measure, in love, because of their work. Make peace among yourselves" (1 Thess 5:12–13). At the same time, for outsiders: "See to it that no one repays another person evil for evil, but always pursue the good, both for one another and for everyone" (5:15). We could offer three observations about this last verse. First, as you can see in table 7.1, Paul's words in 1 Thessalonians 5 are very similar to his words in Romans 12, both of which offer instructions on how to repay evil (words in both passages are underlined).[9]

1 Thess 5:15:	Rom 12:13b, 17:
See to it that <u>no</u> one <u>repays</u> another person <u>evil for evil</u>, but always <u>pursue</u> the good, both for one another and for <u>every</u>one.	<u>pursue</u> hospitality . . . Do <u>not</u> <u>repay</u> anyone <u>evil for evil</u>. Give careful thought for what is good in the sight of <u>all</u> the people.

Table 7.1: Repaying evil

In light of these similarities, it seems that Paul's ideas about hospitality in 57 CE, when he wrote Romans, have not changed dramatically from 50 or 51 CE, when he wrote 1 Thessalonians.

Second, the language of *pursuit* is interesting. *Pursue* translates the Greek word *diōkō*, which, in other contexts, is translated *persecute*. Clearly Paul is not saying "persecute the good" or "persecute hospitality"; that would be absurd. But as we have seen, both 1 Thessalonians and Romans acknowledge that affliction and/or persecution—related but not necessarily the same things—are problems for their respective readers. Both letters flip the language of pursuit/persecution on its head: when others persecute (*diōkō*) Christ's followers, those followers respond by blessing their antagonists and pursuing (*diōkō*) hospitality (per Romans) and "the good" (*agathon*, per 1 Thessalonians).

Third, 1 Thess 5:15 ends using the same phrase we saw in 3:12: *kai eis pantas* ("and for everyone"). That Paul

---

9. "Good" is not underlined because the two texts use different but synonymous words (in 1 Thessalonians, *agathon*, "the good"; in Romans, *kala*, "good things"). Both texts also use slightly different forms of "everyone" (1 Thessalonians: *pantas*; Romans: *pantōn anthrōpōn*; both phrases mean "everyone, all people"). When we take these similarities into consideration, 1 Thess 5:15 and Rom 12:13, 17 are even more alike!

and his co-authors repeatedly return to the idea of hospitality, even using the same wording, suggests this topic is clearly significant. As a point of contrast, perhaps the most common exhortation I hear people repeat from 1 Thessalonians comes from 5:17: "Pray unceasingly." While the word *unceasingly* occurs three times in this letter (see 1 Thess 1:2; 2:13; 5:17), each time in conjunction with some kind of prayer, the authors urge their readers to "pray unceasingly" only once. Unlike this single exhortation to unceasing prayer, the authors urge their readers to pursue *love/the good* for outsiders three times! As important as "pray unceasingly" undoubtedly was for the authors, even more important was their concern for the readers to increase in love and/or pursue the good for hostile, adversarial outsiders.

The theme of hospitality is neither as frequent nor as prominent in 2 Thessalonians, but neither is it absent. At the end of the instructions regarding the "disorderly" (2 Thess 3:6–13), the authors tell their readers: "As for you, brothers and sisters, do not grow weary in doing good" (3:13). The language differs slightly from the wording in 1 Thessalonians.[10] The idea, however, that a Christian's response to a moral problem is to persist in doing good fits right at home with 1 Thessalonians. The next verse takes a harder stance against a disobedient person than anything we saw in 1 Thessalonians ("if anyone does not obey our word through this letter, take note of that person and do not associate with them, so that they might be ashamed"; 2 Thess 3:14). Then again, that harder stance is immediately balanced with an admonition that is perfectly in keeping with 1 Thessalonians' injunctions to hospitality: "Do not regard anyone as an enemy, but consider everyone as a sibling" (2 Thess 3:15).

---

10. Instead of *agathon* for "the good," 2 Thess 3:13 uses the verb *kalopoieō* (*kalos*, "good, beautiful" + *poieō*, "do").

THE FIRST CHRISTIAN LETTERS

HOSPITALITY AS A CONTEMPORARY VIRTUE

Hospitality has been a Christian virtue since the very beginning, which should not be surprising given that hospitality is a virtue in most cultures. For understandable reasons, discussions of hospitality often focus on welcoming people on the margins, such as the poor, the sick, or the otherwise dispossessed. This explains, at least in part, the word *hospital*, in the sense of a medical care facility for the sick or injured. Discussions of hospitality also emphasize welcoming travelers and other kinds of strangers, which explains, at least in part, words like *hostel* and *hotel*.[11] These are all, of course, important aspects of hospitality, and they deserve the extended reflection and discussion they receive.[12] But these are not the kinds of hospitality—Christian or otherwise—that I want to consider for the remainder of this chapter. Neither am I focused on the bourgeois—not bad, but bourgeois—practice of hospitality: the entertainment of guests or visitors, whether friends, acquaintances, or even strangers who are very similar to ourselves. My coworkers may enjoy our hospitality when my wife and I invite them over for dinner and conversation on a weekend, or we may enjoy the hospitality of some friends from our church, and though these are wonderful things to share, they are not the transgressive, risky, open-to-genuine-outsiders kinds of hospitality we saw in Paul's letters.

Paul's ideas about hospitality sprang out of his own experience as the Jewish apostle to the gentiles, "the pagans'

---

11. For discussions of hospitality in the Christian tradition, see Pohl, *Making Room*; Oden, ed., *And You Welcomed Me*; Sutherland, *I Was a Stranger*. I am grateful to my colleague, Sean Ridge, for sharing these resources with me.

12. For a recent discussion of marginalized populations in Paul's letters, see Works, *Least of These*.

apostle," as one scholar has called him.[13] That experience required him to go beyond Jewish spaces in the cities of the eastern Mediterranean basin and to declare to the non-Jewish inhabitants of the spaces he entered that, first, the Jewish God was God not of Jews only but of all nations (see Rom 3:29–30), and second, that Jesus was king not only of Israel but also of the nations. We are used to the idea that Paul entered gentile spaces and proclaimed the gospel. Less familiar, however, is that Paul did not abandon his Jewish identity when entering those spaces. Or, to say the same thing another way, Paul's expression of hospitality did not come at the cost of his Jewishness, as if he could only welcome gentiles or be welcomed by them by being untrue to his tradition and culture and mimicking the tradition and culture of his gentile neighbors.[14] Paul's experience of hospitality left his Jewishness intact; it also left the non-Jewishness of his gentile converts intact. Hospitality respects the identity of both guest and host without compelling either to lose themselves in the identity of the other.

And yet the experience of hospitality is, somehow, transformative; it leaves neither guest nor host unchanged. The Thessalonians, as we have seen, have become *ex-pagan* pagans, gentiles who no longer live or worship like gentiles. The Thessalonians, as everyone up and down the Greek

13. See Fredriksen, *Paul*.

14 It may be objected that in one well-known passage Paul says, "I became as a Jew to the Jews, so that I might win the Jews," and similarly for "those under Torah," "those without Torah" (or "the lawless"; *tois anomois*), and "the weak" (see 1 Cor 9:19–23). Some see here an indication that Paul no longer considers himself a Jew, though under the right conditions he is willing to become or behave "as" (or "like"; *hōs*) a Jew. For alternative readings of this text, which see Paul as unwaveringly Jewish at all times, see Rudolph, *A Jew to the Jews* and Nanos, *Reading Corinthians and Philippians within Judaism* (esp. chap. 3 and 4).

peninsula knows, have "turned to God from idols to serve the living and true God" (1 Thess 1:9), the God of Israel, the God of the Jews who is also the God of all nations. It would be difficult to overstate the significance of this transformation. The Thessalonians have not simply "converted" from one religion to another (or from no religion to Christianity). Their "turning from idols" and forsaking the cultic worship that kept the local gods happy risked those gods' wrath on the local populace. The frequent references to affliction and mistreatment in 1–2 Thessalonians suggest the Thessalonians' families, friends, and neighbors did not look kindly upon this new, bizarre form of worship. Moreover, these gentiles in Thessalonica started to live differently, both from their former lives and from their current neighbors. When Paul and Silvanus and Timothy urge the Thessalonians "to keep control of your self in holiness and honor, not in lustful passion, like the gentiles who do not know God" (1 Thess 4:4–5), they are not necessarily implying any critique of the Thessalonians' current ethical conduct. But they are obviously maligning gentile ethical (and especially sexual) conduct in general.

The Thessalonian Christians remain gentiles, except that they no longer live like gentiles.

If we try to put ourselves in Paul and Silvanus and Timothy's place, this is a difficult balance to maintain. On one hand, they—especially Paul—felt a peculiar call to be "apostle to the gentiles." If Paul and his companions were unwilling to associate with pagans, to receive and be received by gentiles who lived the way gentiles lived, they would be peculiar emissaries to the nations indeed. On the other hand, it would be a mistake to imagine Paul as a first-century street preacher, haranguing passers-by with threats of hellfire and condemnation. The transformation wrought via hospitality is not a transactional, you-are-welcome-if *quid pro quo* that offers itself once certain conditions are met. Hospitality involves welcoming another person *as* an Other person, someone whose life and values and hopes and fears and dreams are reflective of their made-in-the-image-of-God-ness. If we start using our hospitality to gain leverage over an Other, like a carrot dangling from a stick, we are not truly hosts nor is the Other truly a guest.

About a half-century after Paul and his companions wrote 1 Thessalonians, another Jewish author took up his stylus and set himself the task of recording the words and deeds of Jesus as he had heard them from someone he called "the disciple whom Jesus loved." Toward the end of his narrative, he recalls Jesus praying for his followers just hours before his arrest, torture, and execution. "I ask not only on behalf of these," he recounts Jesus saying, before continuing:

> but also on behalf of those who believe in me through their word, that they may all be one. As you, Father, are in me and I am in you, may they also be in us, so that the world may believe that you have sent me. The glory that you have given me I have given them, so that they may be one, as we are one, I in them and you in me, that they may become completely one, so that the world may know that you have sent me and have loved them even as you have loved me. (John 17:20–23 NRSVue)

The prayer for one-ness is not a prayer for same-ness, any more than Jesus and the Father, though one, are the same. Unity—not uniformity, conformity, or compliance, but *unity*—requires hospitality, where different followers of Jesus welcome each other in their difference.

The church with which I am familiar—largely but not solely American; largely but not solely White; largely but not solely Evangelical—has lost sight of this hospitality. In the 1990s we fought over worship styles and music. In the 2000s we fought over the threat or promise of Emergent Christianity. In the 2010s we fought over same-sex marriage and the ordination of openly gay clergy. This last has proven to be especially difficult, with multiple denominations splitting and local congregations disaffiliating from each other over these very important questions. I have views on all these challenges, often quite strong views that I find myself unable to change whether or not I want to. And many of them truly are very important issues. But they are not the *most* important issue. When two people both profess allegiance to Jesus, but they cannot welcome one another because of differences on questions even as important as same-sex marriage or gay ordination, their views on sexuality or marriage have become more fundamental and important to them than their love for Jesus. This failure of hospitality is not simply a result of homophobic bigotry on the Right; open and affirming Christians on the Left are just as susceptible to inhospitality as their traditionalist adversaries.

And Jesus' prayer in John 17 goes unanswered.

What we need, it seems to me, are examples of hospitality, examples that take our breaths away because of their scandalous welcome without cowardly conformity. Examples like that of Daryl Davis, the Black blues musician from Memphis, Tennessee, who was driven by the question, "How can you hate me when you don't even know me?"[15] Daryl began befriending members of America's preeminent White supremacist hate-group, the Ku Klux Klan. His controversial hospitality toward hateful bigots was not always welcomed by other civil rights activists, and for understandable reasons. But Davis's hospitality, motivated by a

15. See Ornstein, *Accidental Courtesy*.

simple desire to know and be known by people predisposed to hate him, has changed real people's hearts.

Perhaps a more intentionally hospitable church—and here I refer to the worldwide church, the body of Christ *en masse*—would have little perceptible difference in a culture that seems so unwilling to welcome others as Others. Perhaps the church—again, I mean the *universal* church—has already lost its ability to influence the culture more broadly. Perhaps our own practice of hospitality, if somehow we were able to recover and restore it, would be too little, too late for a world already marked by crisscrossing battle lines and gathered behind defensive walls.

But so what? Refusing the kind of hospitality Paul envisaged because it would do no good is succumbing to the transactional approach to hospitality we already rejected. We don't, we shouldn't, we *can't* welcome Others because it will change them. We ought, we should, we *must* welcome Others because we have already been changed by the One who welcomed us. Even before we were desirable as guests. Even before we had any hope of returning the favor. We, like the Thessalonians, were invited to Christ's table long before we had any credentials to merit our place at the messianic banquet.

Who do we think we are to refuse others the invitation that changed us?

DISCUSSION QUESTIONS

1. What do you think of the distinction between hospitality aimed inward (i.e., toward people like us, such as family, friends, or people enough like us to make them familiar) versus hospitality aimed outward (i.e., toward others as Others, who are foreign or alien to us, perhaps even offensive)?

2. Who are the kinds of people that traditional churches struggle to welcome? What makes those kinds of people difficult to host? How could the church host them better? What might Pauline hospitality look like for these churches?

3. Who are the kinds of people that progressive churches struggle to welcome? What makes those kinds of people difficult to host? How could the church host them better? What might Pauline hospitality look like for these churches?

4. Who are the kinds of people that you struggle to welcome? What makes those kinds of people difficult to host? How could you host them better? What might Pauline hospitality look like for you?

5. Is there value in hosting people you find offensive, troubling, or otherwise undesirable? What kinds of transformation might this kind of hospitality have for host, guest, or both? Does this kind of hospitality have value if it doesn't transform host, guest, or both?

8

A WORLD UNIMAGINABLE

The Thessalonian Letters as the Word of God

LIKE SO MANY THINGS, the question is subject to considerable debate. Evidence is sparse, in part because the archaeological record is so spotty. But let us say that creatures identifiable as *Homo sapiens* have inhabited the earth for about 200,000 years, perhaps longer, though the stakes are not high if we are wrong. For most of that time, goods, information, and *Homo sapiens* themselves moved, under ideal conditions, as fast as their legs could carry them. At some point, not much more than ten thousand years ago and probably just less than that, *Homo sapiens* began to domesticate certain animals: goats and sheep at first, maybe chickens, and then oxen, asses, horses, and mules. By the time *Homo sapiens* began to move goods or themselves upon animals, we are just over five thousand years in the past.

In other words, if you go outside right now and run as fast as you can down a gentle slope, you will be traveling at or near humanity's top speed for about 195,000 years.

For most of the remaining five thousand years, humanity's top speed remained fairly constant. And slow. Eventually, *Homo sapiens* began to master traveling over water, which was something of a quantum leap in terms of miles per hour. When it came to moving goods and/or personnel, travel by water was significantly faster than over land. But you're still traveling too slowly for a kid to cut the wind with her hand as she wends her way down a river.

Nothing really changed until late-summer, 1830, in the north of England, when George Stephenson and his partners opened the Liverpool and Manchester Railway. The L&MR opened on September 15, 1830, but three weeks earlier, on August 26, Stephenson had arranged an "experimental trip" to display his locomotive, the *Rocket*. Fanny Kemble, at the time a not-yet twenty-one-year-old celebrity and a passenger on Stephenson's *Rocket*, wrote about her experience in a letter:

> [T]he carriage . . . was set off at its utmost speed, thirty-five miles an hour, swifter than a bird flies (for they tried the experiment with a snipe). You cannot conceive what that sensation of cutting the air was; . . . I stood up, and with my bonnet off "drank the air before me." The wind, which was strong, or perhaps the force of our own thrusting against it, absolutely weighed my eyelids down. . . . When I closed my eyes this sensation of flying was quite delightful, and strange beyond description; yet, strange as it was, I had a perfect sense of security, and not the slightest fear.[1]

1. Kemble, *Records of a Girlhood*, 279–86 (p. 283 quoted). Kemble might not have felt so safe if she knew that, less than three weeks later,

Kemble expresses in nearly breathless amazement the top speed her company reached: "thirty-five miles an hour, swifter than a bird flies." In mid-1830, few human beings had traveled so fast. Bicycles, a recent invention, were not capable of such speeds. Short of falling off a very high cliff, getting to 35 mph before 1830 was an impossibility (and no one who managed 35 mph by throwing him- or herself from a cliff is known to have written an account afterward describing the sensation).

In the two hundred years since Kemble won her race with a snipe, *Homo sapiens*'s top speed has only increased. On October 14, 1947, US Air Force test pilot Charles E. "Chuck" Yeager broke the sound barrier for the first time when his experimental Bell X-1 accelerated to 700 mph. Not twenty-two years later, the crew of the Apollo 10 reached the fastest rate of travel for *Homo sapiens* to date: 24,816.1 mph, faster than Stephenson's *Rocket* by a factor of over 709. Again, for about 195,000 years human beings traveled only as fast as our legs could manage. At some point in the last five thousand years, we began to be able to travel as fast as certain animals (especially horses) could carry us. In less than two hundred years, not even 0.1% of the time *Homo sapiens* has been on the earth, we have overtaken the snipe, sound itself, and really anything that can't travel over 24,816 mph.

Granted, only three of us have managed that top speed, and even after three-quarters of a century relatively few human beings have gone faster than the speed of sound. But chances are every one of us first achieved Fanny Kemble's eye-watering velocity on their trip home from the maternity ward, strapped into a bulky, protective car seat,

---

on the very day the L&MR opened, Minister of Parliament William Huskisson would be struck by Stephenson's *Rocket* and die later that night.

surrounded and even overtaken by other, similarly fast-moving human beings. Who among us hasn't fallen asleep traveling at greater than 35 mph (hopefully, someone else was driving)? What Fanny Kemble found remarkable, we don't even notice.

And that's the point. It can be difficult for us to gauge how much the world has changed between any two points in time. During our own lifetimes the world has undergone revolution after revolution, so that life even twenty years ago is difficult to imagine, *and we once lived it*. (At this moment, the iPhone is just past its sixteenth birthday, but how many of us can imagine the world without a smartphone always within reach?) Forty years ago might as well be a remote village in the Chilean Andes; in 1983, cordless telephones had only been on the market for three years, cost about $400 USD, and—if you can imagine—*only made telephone calls*!

If life in Ronald Reagan's United States or Margaret Thatcher's United Kingdom is barely imaginable just four decades later, how much more foreign would be Fanny Kemble's world? What about Martin Luther's pre- or early-Reformation-era Europe? Visigothic Spain? Late pre-Islamic Arabia? These are all nearly incomprehensibly foreign times and places, worlds we can scarcely imagine.

There is a danger we might forget that the world in which Paul lived, only one or two generations into Rome's Imperial Age, is more foreign than we appreciate. As difficult as it is for us to envision Paul's world, Paul could not have conceived in his wildest dreams a world where newborn babies zip home faster than snipes can fly. Not only could Paul not have understood a world where a human being landed on the moon; he would not have been able to wrap his mind around a world capable of *faking* the moon landing. The author of the Thessalonian letters—along with

Silvanus and Timothy, of course—could scarcely consider the world existing beyond the outer limits of his own lifetime. What could this man possibly have to say to the residents of a world beyond his wildest imaginations?

THE FOLLY OF THE BIBLE AS GOD'S ENDURING WORD

The question is, again, subject to considerable debate. Evidence, again, is sparse; again, the archaeological record is spotty. But the collection of texts Christians call "the Old Testament" probably began to take shape early in the post-exilic era, perhaps in the fifth or fourth centuries BCE (500–300 BCE). Books and parts of books are undoubtedly older. Perhaps the book of Amos dates from the eighth century (700s BCE); perhaps the songs of the sea (Exodus 15) or of Deborah (Judges 5) are earlier still. When Paul sat down with Silvanus and Timothy to write to the Thessalonians, his "Bible"—he never used this word; he called his holy writings *graphē*, "writing" or "scripture"—was already hundreds of years old. But when Paul turned to Moses in search of wisdom, he lived in a world that would have been recognizable to Moses. Sure, the sounds of Greek and Latin in places like Egypt and Syria would have been strange. Nevertheless, power in the hands of a single man—called an "emperor" rather than "pharaoh"—or the pervasiveness of peoples who worshiped other gods, or the peculiarity of Israelite (or Judean, or Jewish) worship without idols or images, or myriad other features of the world would have made as much sense to Moses as to Paul.

Both men, however, would have been utterly at sea if they somehow found themselves in the twenty-first century. Travel faster than a snipe? Women participating in public political discourse? Public political discourse? Walmart?!

Not only would these have been as strange to Moses as to Paul; likely neither man would have had a framework for understanding what they were seeing.

Perhaps, then, it is folly for us to turn to writings and traditions from these and other similarly old-fashioned men to help us make sense of our world. Simply put: they never had to wrestle with the social or moral or spiritual questions facing our complex, interconnected societies. If Moses could write—or if it could be written in Moses's name—"When the Lord your God brings you into the land that you are about to enter and occupy and he clears away many nations before you ... and when the Lord your God gives them over to you and you defeat them, then you must utterly destroy them. Make no covenant with them and show them no mercy" (Deut 7:1–2 NRSVue), it is difficult for us to see how this can be wisdom for our own age. Few of us today—hopefully even *none* of us!—would advocate for this as a desirable foreign relations policy. So we who continue to value the Bible as the word of God quietly downplay or neglect such passages and look for wisdom on other pages, like the Ten Commandments (Exod 20:1–17; Deut 5:6–21) or the frequent injunction to care for and provide justice to foreigners, orphans, and widows (e.g., Deut 24:17–22). But is the "benign neglect" of difficult passages or the "cherry-picking" of favored passages really the best way to appropriate the Bible in our own world? Perhaps the most difficult or strange or problematic aspects of our sacred texts do not negate their value and beauty and wisdom. The difficult parts may, instead, invite us to engage the texts, to read them slowly, carefully, in community, and to consider the ways they encourage or challenge or are immaterial for our world.

The key word in that last sentence is *engage*, in the sense of "to deal with, especially at length" or "to give attention to something."[2] It is often easy for too many of us to proclaim our faith in and commitment to the Bible as the word of God without actually reading these complex, cacophonous, foreign texts and wrestling with how they might be made to speak to an equally-but-differently complex and cacophonous present. At the same time, it is often easy for too many of us to unhitch ourselves from the outdated and patriarchal texts of the Bible in favor of "following the Spirit" into a brave new world of equality and justice. Perhaps a humble willingness to put ourselves aside and seek a deep familiarity with this collection of ancient texts might help all of us strike a better balance of being faithful to a tradition that has spanned millennia and addressing the needs of justice and righteousness and integrity in a new and increasingly foreign present.

So, on one hand, it seems to me folly to think any single text or even a collection of texts written in such a foreign world should have anything meaningful to offer us as we chart our way forward as the people of God in our world. On the other hand, I cannot begin to imagine what it would mean "to be the people of God" without some sense of what it has meant in previous generations. So, despite the utter unimaginability of our world to the generations of Abraham's descendants and Jesus' disciples before us, there must be something grounding, anchoring, even *foundational* to these texts that both constrains and enables possibilities for life in this world. Or, to say the same thing differently: if Paul and Silvanus and Timothy could not have imagined the questions we ask of God for this world, perhaps they are also unaffected by the dizzying, dissenting voices that speak at cross-purposes and try to co-opt us into supporting their agendas. Perhaps, if we can take a breath and close our eyes

2. Both phrases come from https://www.merriam-webster.com/dictionary/engage, accessed Aug 6, 2023.

and drown out the noise, these texts can teach us or remind us who we are and what we cherish, before others try to conscript us into their vision of the world and how it should be.

That is, perhaps the folly of these ancient texts as the enduring word of God is the countercultural wisdom we need in a world that has—whether it realizes it or not—lost its way. These letters, and maybe the Bible itself, are less a complex instruction manual for how we should live in a world their authors could not have envisioned and more a fixed point, anchored in something solid even as everything around us seems constantly to shift under our feet. With this in mind, let's briefly survey how the Thessalonian letters might orient us toward our world.

THE ROAD THUS FAR

We began by looking at race and ethnicity in the Thessalonian letters. Neither 1 nor 2 Thessalonians is *about* race or ethnicity, but important racial and/or ethnic dynamics are work in within these letters. The most important one, which is perhaps easily ignored when we approach biblical texts as theological documents and their writers as theologians, is that Paul and Silvanus and Timothy are Jewish authors writing to non-Jewish, gentile, *pagan* readers. At the outset, then, we ought to approach 1–2 Thessalonians, the earliest extant Christian texts, as inter-ethnic communication. These are not simply letters from Christian authors to Christian readers; these letters are part of the mutual incorporation of very different kinds of people—Jews and Macedonians—into a single community. In many ways these different kinds of people maintain their differences in the new community; in other ways they nevertheless identify themselves with each other and claim each other as family (see below).

Paul will later write to other Christians in southern Greece that the Macedonian churches (including the Thessalonians) contributed to a collection for Jewish followers of Jesus in Judea, and they did so "even beyond their means" (2 Cor 8:3 NRSVue). This expression of unity between Jewish and Greek believers is a significant component of Paul's apostolic ministry. At the same time, the ex-pagan Thessalonians have suffered for their faith in Jesus at the hands of their pagan Thessalonian neighbors, and in this way they are like the Jewish believers in Judea who suffer at the hands of other Jews (1 Thess 2:14–16). Our letters do not work out the precise dynamics of these intra- and inter-ethnic dynamics. Even so, we might observe (i) that our Jewish writers do not expect their non-Jewish readers to "Judaize," that is, to live like Jews or to become Jews,[3] and yet (ii) neither did they simply accept that their gentile readers would continue to live as gentiles (see 1 Thess 4:5).

Next we looked at family and familial terms in the Thessalonian letters. Families are the first place we learn how to be human; they provide our earliest social bonds and affect how we bond with others later in life. Despite the very different ethnic identities of Paul and his co-authors, on one hand, and their readers on the other, 1 and 2 Thessalonians draw the authors and their readers into a single family, with multiple relations describing their connection. They are, first and most frequently, *adelphoi*: brothers and sisters, siblings who together addressed the Jewish God of Israel as *our Father*. Rather than be content with being an older brother of sorts, however, Paul and his co-authors also presented themselves as a guiding father of their ex-pagan

3. For a helpful discussion of the difficult term *Judaize(r)*, see Hardin, "Judaizers," in DPL^2 571–74.

children (1 Thess 2:11–12) and, perhaps surprisingly, as a nursing mother, gentle and caring for her infant children (2:7–8).

In our own experiences, perhaps most of us can identify ways that *family* (as a concept) is both a gift and a burden. The dynamics of this gift-and-burden-ness may differ whether we are thinking of our relations with parents, siblings, children, or others (aunts, uncles, cousins, etc.); they may also shift whether we are thinking of ourselves or our relations as burdens or as gifts. Our families place obligations upon us, and obligations are always burdensome. We saw family-as-obligation in the story of Elie Wiesel, wrapped in *tefillin* and praying unthinkable words in an unthinkable place: "With a great love have You loved us." What could possibly provoke someone to utter such preposterous words under—and in defiance of—the banner of *Work Makes One Free*? "My father said [that prayer]," said Wiesel, "his father, his grandfather. How could I be the last?"[4] This is both gift and burden.

In chapter 4 we considered the question of ethics, the "customs or habits" (Greek *ethē*, plural of *ethos*) for the ex-pagan pagans in Thessalonica. The question of moral behavior—what "moral behavior" is, and what makes it moral—is already embedded in a particular narrative framework that relates Creator to creation, cult to conduct, worship to walk. Israel had been called, first and foremost, to "have no other gods before me" (Exod 20:3 NRSVue). When she broke that covenant, one of the closest metaphors to hand for describing her infidelity was adultery: Israel had been a faithless wife, and YHWH an aggrieved husband (see, e.g., Ezekiel 16; Hosea). Adultery (and other forms of sexual immorality) led to broader expressions of injustice and violations of good social relations. Jewish authors could extend

4. Burger, *Witness*, 87.

the link of disordered worship with disordered sexuality to express a critique of pagan religiosity and culture. We see this especially in Wisdom of Solomon 14–15 ("Sexual immorality begins with the idea of idols; their innovation led to the corruption of life"; Wis. 14:12) and in Romans 1. These texts—Ezekiel, Hosea, Wisdom of Solomon, and Romans—all express the connection between worship and sexual desire negatively, but in 1 Thessalonians we see this idea expressed positively: the Thessalonian ex-pagan pagans have "turned to God from idols" (1:9) and now are prepared to pursue what are, for Paul, the keys to virtue: love (*agapē*) and the good (*agathon*).

Sadly, the church today is not quite a beacon of *agapē* or *agathon*-ness in a world looking for such things. Evangelical churches—churches to which I belong, in which I was raised, and with whom I worship and serve—are well-known for taking stances on sex and sexuality as social issues but woefully unresponsive to sexual predation, exploitation, and violence within our own walls. Churches too often appear more concerned to protect their reputation, or their exposure to legal risk, than they are about standing with the victims of sexual abuse and confronting their abusers.[5] The church's support for any kind of sexual ethic—whether traditional, open and affirming, or whatever—will lack all conviction or persuasive power if we are unwilling to confront failures of sexual integrity *within* the church. If the church cannot pursue the good for its least powerful constituents, cannot love its neighbor as itself,

---

5. For a discussion of this issue in the Southern Baptist Convention, see Gross, "Southern Baptist Convention," available at https://www.npr.org/2022/06/02/1102621352/how-the-southern-baptist-convention-covered-up-its-widespread-sexual-abuse-scand (accessed on August 7, 2023). Though this interview concerns the SBC, this problem is not unique to the SBC.

then why should anyone outside the church respect the church's moral authority?

We then turned to questions of eschatology, the doctrine or teaching about last things. Both 1 and 2 Thessalonians have dramatic eschatological moments. In 1 Thessalonians, Paul and Silvanus and Timothy describe Jesus descending out of heaven to earth, with "the dead in Christ" rising to greet him in the air, then also the living in Christ joining them and him to escort him, with his heavenly entourage, back to earth (1 Thess 4:13–18). The whole scene unfolds in much the same way as a distant king or visiting dignitary's arrival (= *parousia*) in a city, as we saw in the accounts of Alexander the Great's arrival in Jerusalem and Paul's arrival in Rome. In 2 Thessalonians, the authors describe an ominous "man of lawlessness," also called a "son of destruction," whose own *parousia* would be heralded by persuasive—but deceptive—signs and wonders, who would solicit for himself the kind of worship and/or cultic devotion appropriate only for the one Creator God of Israel (2 Thess 2:3–12). This latter scenario sounds catastrophic and potentially ruinous, but both letters exhibit a particular concern to encourage the readers to steadfast persistence. Both letters have confidence in God's faithfulness to strengthen and guide the Thessalonians, come what may (see 1 Thess 5:9–11; 2 Thess 2:13–17).

Today, expectations for the future often fall into one of two categories. Some people exhibit an optimistic view in which social activism and the progress of human civilization gradually but inexorably eradicates problems like war, disease, poverty, oppression, and so on. Others offer a pessimistic view in which human culture and society are increasingly depraved and debauched, and only a supernatural intervention like the return of Jesus can set right what has gone so horribly wrong. Both views express a powerful and important truth, but both also neglect an important truth. Yes, we are called to join with God in the work of reconciling all things to himself (Col 1:20) and improving the lives of people in the here and now. But if our vision of the kingdom of God is limited to what can be accomplished by advocating certain economic policies, healthcare reform, antiracism, or whatever, we have a narrow view of the gospel's panoramic vision of the renewal of creation, society, and even our very selves. At the same time, yes, we live always and entirely in a world stamped with the marks of sin, of evil, of brokenness and injustice and wickedness, and we are called to resist the impulses and desires of that world. But if our vision of this world is limited to what has gone wrong, we have missed the goodness God saw in his creation (Genesis 1) and his continuing love even for this imperfect world (e.g., John 3:16). Neither optimism nor pessimism are wrong in themselves, but in both our optimistic and our pessimistic moments, the response of the people of God must be to "do the next right thing."

In chapter 6 we considered the question of 2 Thessalonians' place in the New Testament canon in light of questions about its authorship. Our own cultural moment is especially taken up with questions about "fake news" and the dangers of mis- and disinformation. The early Christians were not unaware of such things; the early centuries of the church saw a flood of texts written in the names of prominent figures, which could lead to debates about the authenticity of some texts.[6] Second Thessalonians is both

---

6. Tertullian, the first church father to write in Latin, opposed Christians who appealed to Paul's example in a second-century text called *The Acts of Paul* to permit women to teach or baptize: "But if certain Acts of Paul, which are falsely so named, claim the example of Thecla for allowing women to teach and to baptize, let men know that in Asia the presbyter who compiled that document, thinking to add of his own to Paul's reputation, was found out, and though he

strikingly similar to and yet, in significant ways, different from 1 Thessalonians. For some readers, the differences between the two letters—especially the tone of 2 Thessalonians vis-à-vis its readers and its eschatological vision—betray it as a pseudepigraphal ("falsely inscribed") letter that was written in the name of, but not by the hand of, Paul (and Silvanus and Timothy). The striking similarities, then, are traces of the actual authors' use of 1 Thessalonians as a model for their text. Perhaps. But it is not unreasonable to flip this logic on its head and to see the similarities between the two letters as betraying the origin of both letters from the apostle and his companions. In this case, the differences would reflect the changed circumstances, new purpose(s), and perhaps not-identical authorial dynamics among the three authors. Unfortunately, the evidence is not conclusive, so we can neither prove nor disprove the Pauline authorship of 2 Thessalonians.

Finally, in chapter 7 we turned to the notion of *philoxenia*, "hospitality." Though the word *philoxenia* does not appear in 1–2 Thessalonians, we can develop a relatively thick description of Pauline hospitality by looking at his words in Romans 12. The ideas there, where Paul does use *philoxenia*, are clearly present in the Thessalonian letters, especially 1 Thessalonians. We saw especially that hospitality is, for Paul, a *transgressive* virtue that crosses the boundaries that separate us from one another. Hospitality is bent both inwardly, to build up the community and nurture its unity, and also outwardly, to welcome the outsider as they are. "See to it that no one repays another person evil for evil," says Paul and Silvanus and Timothy, "but always

---

professed he had done it for love of Paul, was deposed from his position" (Tertullian, *Baptism* 17.5; translation from Evans, ed., *Tertullian's Homily on Baptism*).

pursue the good, both for one another and for everyone" (1 Thess 5:15).

That last phrase, "and for everyone," *kai eis pantas*, perhaps ought to be the Thessalonian letters' most trumpeted contribution to Christian theology and practice: an invitation and welcome to others *as Others*. But this kind of welcome is not easy, neither is it uncontroversial. Conservative and progressive churches alike have clear ideas about the kinds of people who are or should be worthy of our hospitality and, conversely, the kinds of people who are not. I can think of both individuals and types of persons I would prefer not to see in my local church. But that's the problem, right? It's not *my* church. The table on which we place the body and the blood of Christ is not *my* table. My desire to control access and manage participation is a sign of my lack of faith that God can work in the lives of people different from me. This is an attitude both common in the church and contrary to the gospel.

FINAL WORDS

We began by acknowledging that, for many of us, the Thessalonian letters have been more like junk mail in our Bibles, the theological equivalent of unsolicited credit card offers or requests for donations. Until very recently, I hadn't felt the need to pay very much attention to these letters, except perhaps for the interesting fact that one of them was likely the oldest book in the New Testament. The Thessalonian letters were easy to ignore, and I was happy to do so. It helps that they are short, but my neglect of Leviticus and Revelation proves I am more than capable of ignoring much longer texts.

So what happens if we read Paul's letters, especially 1–2 Thessalonians, not just as writings from a first-century

Jewish emissary on behalf of the Jewish God to non-Jewish peoples, but also as scripture, as the word of God for us, letters that tell us who we are, what we are, and point us toward who and what we might be?

- For those of us who, like Paul's imagined readers, are not Jews by birth (see 1 Thess 1:9), these letters fold us—perhaps we could say *naturalize* us—into the nation of God's people, non-Jews who join with Israel in worship of her covenantal God even as we maintain our own distinctive identifies as gentiles, as ex-pagan peoples.
- For those of us who, like Paul and his coauthors, are Jews by birth (see Gal 2:15), these letters provide a model for making space for the ethnic Other who joins us in worship of our covenantal God and for participating in the work of reconciling all things to himself (see 2 Cor 5:16–21).
- These letters express our adoption into the family of this God and his people, nurtured and cared for and connected to what another author once called "a great cloud of witnesses" (Heb 12:1). These have sought—imperfectly yet faithfully—to walk with the Creator God and to extend his goodness and love throughout his creation, to everyone who believes "and for everyone" (*kai eis pantas*), and we, as their fictive if not their factual descendants, walk a similarly impossible path, unwilling that we should be the last.
- We have seen Paul advocate an ethic of *agapē* (love) and *agathon* (the good), which is not a "law-free" gospel uninterested in the behavior of its converts. Paul's moral expectations for his readers are quite high; in Paul's world and in our own, neither love nor goodness is easy or comes naturally.

- We have found in these letters a recognition that the present state of the world is in opposition to God and his reign, that there are indeed children of the night and of darkness (see 1 Thess 5:5–7), and so a Pollyanna hope for the future is unwisely naïve. At the same time, the present state of the world is also the site of God's creative and restorative activity even among "the gentiles who do not know God" (4:5), and so a fatalistic renunciation of the future is unlovingly cynical.

- These letters, including the disputed 2 Thessalonians, offer us an ideal vision of ourselves, in which we are encouraged and strengthened by Jesus himself as well as by our God and Father, empowered for "every good work and word" (2 Thess 2:16–17). Rather than refusing their vision of me because of their failures to live up to it, I find myself hoping beyond hope that I might somehow embody their vision. I also hope later generations will look at me graciously and with compassion as they see the obvious ways I fell short, as they certainly will.

- Perhaps most compellingly, in light of my own temptation to evaluate previous generations critically and my own fear of how future generations will evaluate me, these letters offer us a vision of hospitality that is both scandalous and transformative. In the kingdom of heaven, after the *shofar* (trumpet) blows and the Lord descends and we escort him back to a renewed world where he is Lord, perhaps we will experience a trans- or even pan-generational hospitality. If so, perhaps the task in the present is to anticipate that experience by extending a universal invitation to a table that is not ours.

THE FIRST CHRISTIAN LETTERS

* * *

Imagine yourself in 1830, seated next to Fanny Kemble, waiting for George Stephenson's *Rocket* to lurch into motion. In this moment, she cannot imagine the exhilaration of traveling at thirty-five miles per hour, the feel of the air and the wind at her face. Would you try to explain what lies in store for her? The sense of being tossed to one side as the train bends to the left or to the right? The steady, rhythmic feel of the engine driving the locomotive's pistons and turning its wheels? The flashing of shadow as trees and cliffs and houses pass by? Or would you sit silently, knowing what she cannot know until she experiences it for herself?

I wonder if 1 and 2 Thessalonians are bit like Paul trying to explain to mere pedestrians how it feels to travel faster than the birds. Perhaps reading these letters will always fall short of experiencing life in the kingdom of God. But perhaps these letters can spark our imagination for what that kingdom *could* be like, its potential and possibility. Perhaps these letters can spur us to do God's will, "on earth as it is in heaven."

At the very least, perhaps these letters can cause us to grow and increase in love for one another. And for everyone.

DISCUSSION QUESTIONS

1. If you had to justify the presence of 1–2 Thessalonians in the Bible, what would you say? Should these letters be left in the canon? Should we consider removing one or both? What might we lose if we did? What might we gain if we keep them?

2. Did any part of our discussion of 1–2 Thessalonians resonate with you or pique your interest? What did

you find helpful for your own efforts at being the people of God in this world?

3. As you read 1–2 Thessalonians for yourself, was there anything missing for our discussion in this book? What in Paul and Silvanus and Timothy's letters did we ignore or neglect that you would like to have seen considered?
4. If Paul and Silvanus and Timothy wrote 1–2 Thessalonians to you, how would you reply? What would you write back? What would you say?

WORKS CITED

Alexander, Loveday. "Ancient Book Production and the Circulation of the Gospels." In *The Gospels for All Christians: Rethinking the Gospel Audiences*, edited by Richard Bauckham, 71–112. Grand Rapids: Eerdmans, 1998.

———. *The Preface to Luke's Gospel: Literary Convention and Social Context in Luke 1.1-4 and Acts 1.1*. SNTSMS 78. Cambridge: Cambridge University Press, 1993.

Anderson, Benedict. *Imagined Communities: Reflections on the Origin and Spread of Nationalism*. Rev. ed. London: Verso, 2006.

Ascough, Richard S. *1&2 Thessalonians: An Introduction and Study Guide: Encountering the Christ Group at Thessalonike*. T. & T. Clark Study Guides to the New Testament. London: T. & T. Clark, 2014.

———. *Paul's Macedonian Associations: The Social Context of Philippians and 1 Thessalonians*. WUNT 2/161. Tübingen: Mohr Siebeck, 2003.

Beck, Richard. *Unclean: Meditations on Purity, Hospitality, and Mortality*. Eugene, OR: Cascade, 2011.

Bishop, Bill. *The Big Sort: Why the Clustering of Like-Minded America Is Tearing Us Apart*. Boston: Mariner, 2008.

Bloom, Paul. *Just Babies: The Origins of Good and Evil*. New York: Broadway, 2013.

Boring, M. Eugene. *I and II Thessalonians: A Commentary*. NTL. Louisville, KY: Westminster John Knox, 2015.

Brookins, Timothy A. *First and Second Thessalonians*. PCNT. Grand Rapids: Baker Academic, 2021.

Brown, Donald E. "Human Universals, Human Nature and Human Culture." *Daedalus* 133.4 (2004) 47–54.

Buell, Denise Kimber. *Why This New Race? Ethnic Reasoning in Early Christianity*. New York: Columbia University Press, 2005.

Burger, Ariel. *Witness: Lessons from Elie Wiesel's Classroom*. Boston: Houghton Mifflin Harcourt, 2018.

Carney, Timothy P. *Alienated America: Why Some Places Thrive While Others Collapse*. New York: Harper, 2019.

Charlesworth, James H. "Why Should Experts Ignore Acts in Pauline Research?" In *The Early Reception of Paul the Second Temple Jew: Text, Narrative and Reception History*, edited by Isaac W. Oliver and Gabriele Boccaccini, 151–66. LSTS 92. London: T. & T. Clark, 2019.

Damasio, Antonio. *The Strange Order of Things: Life, Feeling, and the Making of Cultures*. New York: Pantheon, 2018.

Elliott, J. K., ed. *The Apocryphal New Testament: A Collection of Apocryphal Christian Literature in an English Translation*. Oxford: Oxford University Press, 1993.

Elliott, John H. *A Home for the Homeless: A Social-Scientific Criticism of 1 Peter, Its Situation and Strategy*. Minneapolis: Fortress, 1990.

———. "The Rehabilitation of an Exegetical Step-Child: 1 Peter in Recent Research." *JBL* 95 (1976) 243–54.

Evans, Ernest, ed. *Tertullian's Homily on Baptism*. London: SPCK, 1964.

Foot, Philippa. "The Problem of Abortion and the Doctrine of the Double Effect." *Oxford Review* 5 (1967) 5–15.

Fredriksen, Paula. *Paul: The Pagans' Apostle*. New Haven, CT: Yale University Press, 2017.

———. "What Does It Mean to See Paul 'within Judaism'?" *JBL* 141 (2022) 359–80.

Gallagher, Edmon L., and John D. Meade. *The Biblical Canon Lists from Early Christianity: Texts and Analysis*. Oxford: Oxford University Press, 2017.

Gamble, Harry Y. *Books and Readers in the Early Church: A History of Early Christian Texts*. New Haven, CT: Yale University Press, 1995.

Gaventa, Beverly Roberts. *Our Mother Saint Paul*. Louisville, KY: Westminster John Knox, 2007.

Goldberg, Jonah. *Suicide of the West: How the Rebirth of Tribalism, Populism, Nationalism, and Identity Politics Is Destroying American Democracy*. New York: Crown Forum, 2018.

Gorman, James L., Jeff W. Childers, and Mark W. Hamilton, eds. *Slavery's Long Shadow: Race and Reconciliation in American Christianity*. Grand Rapids: Eerdmans, 2019.

Gray, Patrick. "Apocryphal Pauline Literature." In *DPL*² 42–46.

———. *Opening Paul's Letters: A Reader's Guide to Genre and Interpretation*. Grand Rapids: Baker Academic, 2012.

Gross, Terry. "How the Southern Baptist Convention Covered Up Its Widespread Sexual Abuse Scandal." *Fresh Air*. NPR, 2 June 2022.

Gupta, Nijay K. *1 and 2 Thessalonians*. Zondervan Critical Introductions to the New Testament. Grand Rapids: Zondervan Academic, 2019.

———. "Ethics." In *DPL*² 279–88.

Haidt, Jonathan. *The Happiness Hypothesis: Finding Modern Truth in Ancient Wisdom*. New York: Basic, 2006.

Hardin, Justin K. "Judaizers." In *DPL*² 571–74.

Hodge, Caroline E. Johnson. *If Sons, Then Heirs: A Study of Kinship and Ethnicity in the Letters of Paul*. Oxford: Oxford University Press, 2007.

Jones, Ivor H. "Music and Musical Instruments: Musical Instruments." In *ABD* 4:934–39.

Kemble, Fanny. *Records of a Girlhood*. New York: Henry Holt, 1884.

Levine, Amy-Jill, and Marc Zvi Brettler. *The Bible with and without Jesus: How Jews and Christians Read the Same Stories Differently*. San Francisco: HarperOne, 2020.

Malherbe, Abraham J. *The Letters to the Thessalonians: A New Translation with Introduction and Commentary*. AB 32B. New York: Doubleday, 2000.

———. *Paul and the Thessalonians: The Philosophic Tradition of Pastoral Care*. Philadelphia: Fortress, 1987.

Nanos, Mark D. *Reading Corinthians and Philippians within Judaism*. Eugene, OR: Cascade, 2017.

Oden, Amy G., ed. *And You Welcomed Me: A Sourcebook on Hospitality in Early Christianity*. Nashville: Abingdon, 2001.

Ornstein, Matthew, dir. *Accidental Courtesy: Daryl Davis, Race and America*. First Run Features, 2016.

Orwell, George. *The Road to Wigan Pier*. London: Gollancz, 1937.

Pohl, Christine D. *Making Room: Recovering Hospitality as a Christian Tradition*. Grand Rapids: Eerdmans, 1999.

Putnam, Robert D. *Bowling Alone: The Collapse and Revival of American Community*. New York: Simon & Schuster, 2000.

Riesner, Rainer. *Paul's Early Period: Chronology, Mission Strategy, Theology*. Translated by Doug Stott. Grand Rapids: Eerdmans, 1998.

Rodríguez, Rafael. *If You Call Yourself a Jew: Reappraising Paul's Letter to the Romans*. Eugene, OR: Cascade, 2014.

———. *Jesus Darkly: Remembering Jesus with the New Testament*. Nashville: Abingdon, 2018.

Rodríguez, Rafael, and Matthew Thiessen, eds. *The So-Called Jew in Paul's Letter to the Romans*. Minneapolis: Fortress, 2016.

Rollens, Sarah E. "Paul, 1 Thessalonians." In *Brill Encyclopedia of Early Christianity*, edited by David G. Hunter, Paul J. J. van Geest, and Bert Jan Lietaert Peerbolte. Leiden: Brill, 2022. Online. http://dx.doi.org/10.1163/2589-7993_EECO_SIM_036442.

Rosling, Hans, Anna Rosling Rönnlund, and Ola Rosling. *Factfulness: Ten Reasons We're Wrong about the World—and Why Things Are Better Than You Think*. New York: Flatiron, 2018.

Rudolph, David J. *A Jew to the Jews: Jewish Contours of Pauline Flexibility in 1 Corinthians 9:19–23*. 2nd ed. Eugene, OR: Pickwick, 2016.

Saad, Layla F. *Me and White Supremacy: Combat Racism, Change the World, and Become a Good Ancestor*. Naperville, IL: Sourcebooks, 2020.

Sabar, Ariel. *Veritas: A Harvard Professor, a Con Man and the Gospel of Jesus's Wife*. New York: Doubleday, 2020.

Smith, James K. A. *Desiring the Kingdom: Worship, Worldview, and Cultural Formation*. Grand Rapids: Baker Academic, 2009.

Stern, Menahem. *Greek and Latin Authors on Jews and Judaism*. 3 vols. Jerusalem: Israel Academy of Sciences and Humanities, 1976–84.

Sutherland, Arthur. *I Was a Stranger: A Christian Theology of Hospitality*. Nashville: Abingdon, 2006.

Thiessen, Matthew. "Construction of Gentiles in the Letter to the Ephesians." In *The Early Reception of Paul the Second Temple Jew: Text, Narrative and Reception History*, edited by Isaac W. Oliver and Gabriele Boccaccini, 13–25. LSTS 92. London: T. & T. Clark, 2019.

———. *Jesus and the Forces of Death: The Gospels' Portrayal of Ritual Impurity within First-Century Judaism*. Grand Rapids: Baker Academic, 2020.

———. *A Jewish Paul: The Messiah's Herald to the Gentiles*. Grand Rapids: Baker Academic, 2023.

Thiselton, Anthony C. *1 and 2 Thessalonians through the Centuries*. Blackwell Bible Commentaries. Malden, MA: Wiley-Blackwell, 2011.

Tucker, J. Brian, and Coleman A. Baker, eds. *T. & T. Clark Handbook to Social Identity in the New Testament*. London: Bloomsbury T. & T. Clark, 2014.

Works Cited

Vermes, Geza. *The Complete Dead Sea Scrolls in English.* Rev. ed. London: Penguin, 2004.

Wanamaker, Charles A. *The Epistles to the Thessalonians.* NIGTC. Grand Rapids: Eerdmans, 1990.

Watts, Marina. "In Smithsonian Race Guidelines, Rational Thinking and Hard Work Are White Values." *Newsweek*, 17 July 2020, § Culture. https://www.newsweek.com/smithsonian-race-guidelines-rational-thinking-hard-work-are-white-values-1518333.

Weatherly, Jon A. "The Authenticity of 1 Thessalonians 2:13–16: Additional Evidence." *JSNT* 13 (1991) 79–98.

White, Benjamin L. "The Pauline Tradition." In *T. & T. Clark Handbook to the Historical Paul*, edited by Ryan S. Schellenberg and Heidi Wendt, 39–53. London: T. & T. Clark, 2022.

Works, Carla Swafford. *The Least of These: Paul and the Marginalized.* Grand Rapids: Eerdmans, 2020.

www.ingramcontent.com/pod-product-compliance
Lightning Source LLC
Chambersburg PA
CBHW030112170426
43198CB00009B/599